THE SECRET OF THE TAROT

How The Story of the Cathars was Concealed in the Tarot of Marseilles

ROBERT SWIRYN

Published by Pau Hana Publishing.
P.O. Box 1409
Kapaa, HI 96746
U.S.A.
web: http://www.thesecretofthetarot.com

Printed in the United States by CreateSpace.
To order additional copies go to www.createspace.com/900000326.

ISBN: 0615304389
ISBN-13: 9780615304380
Library of Congress Control Number: 2010938064

Unthinking respect for authority is the worst enemy of truth.

—Albert Einstein

Acknowledgements

∽

I would like to thank the following people for their help and support in the production of this book: First, to my wife, Darcy, for all her help and unwavering support, from the initial concept to the final result. To Barbara Ardinger, for her professional editing and for urging me to continue to write and rewrite—and then rewrite again. To my daughter, Carla, for her time, keen insight and valuable commentary. To Wil Welsh, for his encouragement and suggestions along the way. To all the individuals involved in helping me acquire the images contained in the book, including Bobbie Bensaid of U.S. Games Systems, Inc., and Alison Stones, PhD, FSA, of the Department of History of Art and Architecture, University of Pittsburgh, for her fine photographic work on the French cathedrals of Notre Dame de Chartres and St. Sernin. To Francine Kanter, for her help in translating the necessary correspondence with my French sources. To Mary, Huck, Bernice, Rosanne and everyone else who participated in our lively discussions at the Aeclectic Tarot forum. Also to Jean-Michel David of the Association of Tarot Studies, and Lothar of trionfi.com, for all the helpful feedback. Finally, to the staff at CreateSpace for their services in the design and final creation of this book.

Contents

∽

A Brief Timeline

1145 - Bernard of Clairvaux travels to Languedoc to preach against heresy.

1167 - Bishop Nicetas attends the Council of Saint-Felix.

1194 - Raymond VI succeeds his father as Count of Toulouse.

1198 - Pope Innocent III is elected.

1207 - Raymond VI is excommunicated by the pope.

1208 - Peter of Castelnau, the pope's legate, is murdered by one of Raymond's vassals. Raymond is indicted for the crime.

1209 - Beginning of the Albigensian Crusade.

1215 - The Fourth Lateran Council in Rome restates the Church's stand against heresy.

1216 - Simon de Montfort is granted the title of Lord of Languedoc. Pope Innocent III dies and is succeeded by Honorius III. Confirmation of the Dominican order of preachers.

1218 - Simon de Montfort is killed in the siege of Toulouse.

1222 - Raymond VI dies and is succeeded by his son, Raymond VII.

1223 - Louis VIII succeeds his father, Philip II.

1226 - Louis VIII dies and is succeeded by his twelve-year-old son, Louis IX. The affairs of the crown are managed by his mother, Blanche of Castile.

1229 - Raymond VII surrenders to Louis IX.

1233 - The Inquisition is established in Toulouse.

1244 - Montsegur falls. Two hundred and ten Cathars are burned in a mass fire at the base of the castle.

1249 - Raymond VII dies at age 52.

1270 - Raymond's daughter, Joan, and her husband, Alphonse, die childless, leaving Toulouse to France.

Preface

෮

I have been intrigued with the pictures in the tarot for sometime, not out of a desire to read fortunes, but simply because I find them interesting in the way they represent a spiritual art form. It was not until I became familiar with the history of medieval France that I discovered what they really had to say.

The deck which attracted me the most was the one referred to as the Tarot of Marseilles. This early form of the tarot was printed between the fifteenth and seventeenth centuries and maintains a classical look. By comparison, modern versions of the tarot seem to have drifted away from a sense of historical authenticity. At some deeper level, the cards of the Tarot of Marseilles seem to have a story to tell, as if a part of history had been frozen within its images—a story which others might rediscover at a later time.

Along with my interest in the tarot, I began to develop a fascination with medieval history. Like millions of others, my imagination was stirred after reading books like *Holy Blood, Holy Grail* and Dan Brown's, *The Da Vinci Code*. As I began to read more about the Crusades, the Knights Templar, and other related topics, I stumbled onto a subject which particularly caught my attention. This concerned a religious group called the *Cathari* (or Cathars) who became a dominant influence during the twelfth and thirteenth centuries in what is now southern France. The Cathars were considered heretics by the Roman Catholic Church and were viciously persecuted during the Albigensian Crusade of 1209-1229 and by the Inquisition, which was set up to continue the elimination of heresy in the area. The efficiency of these operations was such that the Cathars were thought to be completely wiped out.

As I continued to investigate this subject, I began to recognize connections between the historical characters and events of this period of time and the images in the tarot cards. In addition to retelling the story of the Cathar saga, the spiritual messages of the Cathars also seemed to have found their place in the cards. Each book I read on the subject inadvertently revealed additional insights into the symbolism of the tarot. It was as if the pieces of a puzzle were coming together. Surely, I thought, these associations couldn't be purely coincidental. The anticipation of finding additional clues made me feel like an amateur detective on a historical case.

What eventually appeared evident to me was that someone, or some group may have devised a plan to use the Tarot of Marseilles as a secret instructional vehicle to preserve the story of the Cathar persecution. Basically, this would serve two purposes. First, it would record for posterity the events of the Albigensian Crusade from the point of view of those who fought to protect themselves from the invading forces of the north. Second, it would allow the spiritual messages of the Cathars to be passed on in a covert, underground system of communication undetected by the Church. But these connections in the tarot went beyond the broad topic of Catharism. It included specific details of people like Count Raymond VI of Toulouse, Simon de Montfort, Blanche of Castille, Pope Innocent III and others who played a significant role in the events of the time.

It was surprising to think that no one had seen this connection before. But I soon discovered that several notable tarot historians had already suggested a similar link between the tarot and the heretical sects of the Middle Ages. A few even mentioned the Cathars by name. In his book, *The Tarot*, for example, Alfred Douglas writes, "It has been suggested that the Tarot cards might have been produced by Cathars as a means of representing their doctrines pictorially to those who were illiterate."[1] However, no one, to my knowledge, has actually attempted to describe the details in the images of the individual cards in this historical context. This is the gap this book intends to fill. In the pages ahead, we will explore some of the characters who played a part in these events and some of the spiritual messages of the Cathars in order to reveal how this page of history became secretly concealed within the Tarot of Marseilles.

I understand that some of the ideas I am presenting in this book conflict with the accepted theories of many tarot readers and historians. I also understand that an attempt to prove any theory of the tarot beyond question is futile. No one in the past has been able to accomplish such an explanation to everyone's satisfaction. As odd as it may seem, after six centuries, there is no universally accepted explanation of the meaning of the tarot cards. This has lent the tarot to a wide array of interpretation which has been fuel for debate for some and an occupation for others. To this scope of proposed interpretations, this book presents another explanation—an alternative viewpoint, if you will.

My intention is to present a picture which may stimulate one's imagination and unlock further interest in the history and evolution of the tarot. I ask only that the reader begin with an open mind and withhold his or her final opinion until the end of the book. In many instances, I borrow the words of those who have established themselves as experts in this field in order to substantiate certain points. To the extent that I have stimulated the reader's curiosity, or that he or she can take from this book a new way of looking at the cards, I will have accomplished my goal.

It should be made clear from the beginning that this book is not about divination or fortune telling, nor is it about how to read a tarot spread. Numerous authors have already offered sufficient advice in that area. Many writers on the tarot have presented a psychological or occult interpretation of the cards— often associating them with visions of the soul's journey through its various stages of spiritual growth. Although these adventures in divination may be interesting to many people, they do little to reveal the original intent of the artists. What is presented here is an attempt to discover what the creators of the Tarot of Marseilles had in mind when they designed their cards—secrets which I believe we can find by exploring their historical context.

It is not within the scope of this book to present a complete analysis of the tarot or to review all the existing theories regarding its origins. That task in itself could easily fill a hefty volume. For those interested in learning more about the various theories of the tarot's development, I would refer them to the writings of Robert O'Neill, Stuart Kaplan, Michael Dummett, and others who have already provided us with comprehensive reviews of the subject. I present here only a brief discussion of the tarot's evolution into the Marseilles decks along with a look at the Cathars of Languedoc as a background to help our understanding of the story. In the process of presenting this background, we will become familiar with the major players of the Albigensian Crusade and the spiritual beliefs of the Cathars, which we will see incorporated into the symbolism of the tarot. Along the way, we will take clues from their culture and history, and from the language they used.

Many of the images referred to in this book are from the Nicolas Conver Tarot by Heron. This is probably the most famous of the Marseilles decks. Conver started his own factory in Marseilles in the mid-eighteenth century and was awarded the title of "master Cartier in Marseilles, engraver in the King's court."[2] There are other Marseilles-style cards which predate the Conver deck, such as those of Jean Dodal and Jean Noblet (circa 1660), which differ slightly in a few instances. However, all of the Marseilles decks are adopted from earlier editions of the tarot (such as the fifteenth-century Cary sheet) and all exhibit a basic similarity. Unfortunately, most of these earlier cards were either destroyed or lost. Although the "official" Tarot of Marseilles became popular after Louis XIII authorized the printing of playing cards in Marseilles in 1631, we can assume that their original inspiration came from these earlier decks.

Introduction

෨

*I will give you the keys of the Kingdom of Heaven, and
whatever you bind on earth shall be bound in heaven.*

Matthew 16:19

The spirit of a culture is often reflected in its art. To the extent
this holds true, the culture of medieval Europe can be described
as one of deep religious faith—for the art of the Middle Ages
is overwhelmingly religious in nature. In one respect, religious
art served as a way for the Church to educate a largely illiterate
population. It was a time when pictures and symbols were used
to speak to the mind and the soul. Emile Mâle has said, "It is
evident that medieval art was before all things a symbolic art, in
which form is used mainly as the vehicle of spiritual meaning."[3]
Religious images on the walls of churches depicting themes
from the Bible served as visual textbooks of morality for those
seeking spiritual instruction. In addition to religious images
from the New and Old Testaments—which can still be seen in
the architecture of hundreds of cathedrals throughout Europe—
depictions of the zodiac and mundane labors reminded the
faithful when to harvest and perform other work necessary to
sustain life in a harsh world.

In the same light, other forms of medieval art may have
had a similar tutorial function. In the case of the tarot, the
artwork of the major arcana—the twenty two picture cards

1

which were added to a four-suited card game—leaves a wealth of questions as to its meaning and purpose. If we are to consider these illustrations as the intentional expressions of medieval artists, and not as purely random or arbitrary images, then we must attempt to discover, within the culture of the time, their true meaning. Originally, the artists of the major arcana may have included images to please their aristocratic patrons. As the tarot transitioned through the modern era, it took on a more occult theme. But during its early evolution into the Tarot of Marseilles—a product which matured in seventeenth-century France—the tarot experienced changes which may have been influenced more by the significant historical events which influenced the people of the area. It is this historical connection with which this book is concerned.

The tarot is one of the most mysterious systems of art known to man. Since its introduction in fifteenth-century Europe, it has passed through many alterations and reinterpretations. Modern decks of tarot cards have been created that, in many cases, hardly resemble the sources from which they originated. The tarot has survived hundreds of years, not only as a game, but also as a tool for divination and the occult. But regardless of changes to the tarot, the proof of its longevity lies to a large extent in the universality of its images and in the fact that those images tend to speak in a language that many people find transcendent of one particular place or time. It is this same mystical and universal quality that makes the tarot a clever vehicle for disguising its heretical messages.

The variations of the history of the tarot are as shrouded in as much uncertainty as the interpretations of its symbolism. Experts in the field of the tarot have presented a wide variety of theories of its origins and the meanings of its symbols. Some writers have placed the origins of the cards with the Egyptians; some with the Persians. Others link it to the Kabbalah, making a connection between the twenty-two letters of the Hebrew alphabet, the twenty two paths linking the *sepherot* (stages) of the tree of life, and the twenty two cards of the major arcana. Some see the significance of astrology in the cards, based on the appearance of zodiacal images and the fact that astrology was one of the major sciences of the Middle Ages. Still others believe that the tarot was brought to Europe by the gypsies who were once believed to have carried ancient wisdom with them in their travels through Europe. However, none of these theories have been universally accepted. In such a diverse assortment of opinions, it might be helpful to keep our attention focused on the historical environment from which the tarot evolved. In this way, we might get closer to discovering the actual source from which the cards speak.

During the twelfth and thirteenth centuries, Europe was beginning to come out of a period of suppressed intellectualism and individualism which we commonly refer to as the Dark Ages. The Roman Catholic Church controlled the production of nearly all written material and didn't hesitate to ban anything that was considered a challenge to its own teachings. However, some progressive thinkers were beginning to question the platitudes of the Church as they explored the natural sciences. The twelfth century saw the rise of the universities, which taught

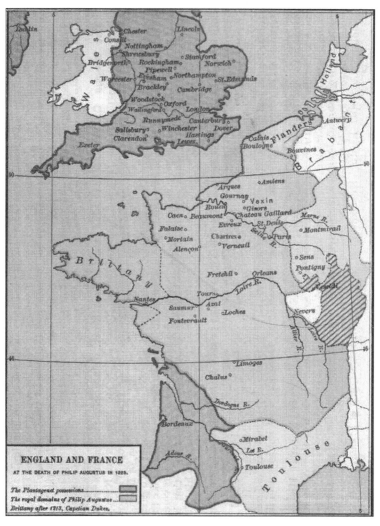

Map of France in 1223, courtesy of Jane Vadnal.

the works of Aristotle along with the core subjects of grammar, rhetoric, astrology, and mathematics. Along with this rise in intellectualism came a broader search for answers to religious questions. Donald Logan explains that the twelfth century saw "a religious enthusiasm seldom, perhaps never, witnessed before in the (by then) long history of Christianity."[4] In the third of a series of books on Christian mysticism, Bernard McGinn tells us that "The early medieval opposition to change, the myth that what is old is good and what is new must be bad, had come under increasing question during the twelfth and thirteenth centuries, especially in relation to the formation of new religious orders."[5] The Franciscan and Dominican orders are examples of two groups that expanded the role of the orthodox priesthood by establishing a monastic lifestyle in the footsteps of their founders, Francis of Assisi and Dominic Guzman. However, others, in search of what it meant to live as true Christians, questioned some of the fundamental institutions and went outside the guidelines of the Church to find their answers. They were, of course, declared to be heretics by Rome.

As early as the eleventh century, Western Europe was seeing these heretical sects growing in number. Many people, disillusioned by the abuses of the Church, were converted to alternative religious views by wandering preachers who offered messages of hope, belonging, and salvation. The Cathars, predominant in Italy and France, were one such group. One difference which set the Cathars apart from some of the other groups that challenged the Catholic Church was the fact that they presented an alternative theology supported by their own organization with their own priests, churches, and dioceses. Due to their success in converting their countrymen and women, the number of Cathars in southern France, known then as Languedoc, grew to a point where they became a threat to the authority of Rome. Although some towns remained Catholic by majority, others—where support from the nobility allowed greater religious tolerance—were known to be inhabited largely by the Cathar faithful. Attempts to convert the heretics back into the fold were basically unsuccessful. Finally, in 1209, Pope Innocent III persuaded the French crown to answer his call for a holy crusade against the people of this region, often referred to as the Albigensians. Innocent urged his crusaders to "attack the followers of heresy more fearlessly even than the Saracens, since they are more evil .... Let pious zeal inspire you to avenge this monstrous crime against your God."[6] After twenty years of brutal war, followed by decades of persecution by the Inquisition, the once peaceful Cathars were all but annihilated from the face of the earth. Most historians accept the fact that their teachings shared the same fate.

However, some survivors fled their homes and went to live in remote, mountainous regions that offered a degree of safety. There is also evidence that many refugees found protection in towns and cities in Italy, where they were shown greater acceptance by some of the powerful patrons there. Wakefield tells us that "in Italian cities the political situation gave Catharism greater security, and it retained its vitality there for decades after it was dying out elsewhere."[7] Given their dire situation, it would seem only natural that these

Cathar survivors would seek a way to preserve their teachings in which they believed so passionately, although in a more underground fashion.

At first, they may have passed on these messages orally, as was the customary tradition, to those willing to listen. Eventually, a memory system must have been developed and used to make the dissemination of their information more efficient. In *The Devil's Picture Book*, Paul Huson explains that the occult principle behind a deck of tarot cards may owe a lot to monasticism, "if not for originating it, then at least for preserving it." For the medieval monk, memory served a far greater purpose than it does for us nowadays. All books consisted of laboriously hand-written manuscripts. Indeed, the art of writing itself was rare and mnemonic systems similar to those seen today were very much in demand. "The simplest type of such a memory system consists of a series of pictorial images, usually arranged in some special order, which may be used as a mental filing index or pigeonhole rack. The medieval student monk could, by vividly visualizing each portion of the tract he wished to learn, file the section away in one of his memory boxes."[8] Since the written word belonged almost exclusively to a small educated class, mostly clerical by profession, the larger masses of people would need a system that could be conveyed visually. Hiding their teachings within the images of the Italian and then the French tarot cards may have been the perfect vehicle for this purpose. In this way, it is very possible that, although unintentional, the teaching methods of the monasteries of the Middle Ages helped in the development of the tarot system.

In a similar fashion, each card of the tarot's major arcana could have been used to elicit specific historical events and selected teachings put to memory and repeated over and over in the traditional art of storytelling. Like a set of flash cards, the tarot would reveal its hidden messages as each card was turned up. Cynthia Giles writes that "groups possessing esoteric knowledge may well have gone underground to preserve their lives and lore; the Tarot images could have been created as memory aids or meditational devices by one of these groups.... In any case, as long as the Tarot trumps were part of a game, their symbolic significance was effectively concealed."[9]

To avoid detection by the Church, the tarot's heretical messages would have to be well disguised. And to accomplish this, the information was well concealed in the common images of medieval art. In addition, parody, symbolism, and allegory were introduced, just as is sometimes done in our modern political cartoons. The true meaning of the card's images would be known only to those who were privy to its secrets.

Any exploration of the real meaning of the tarot, however, becomes a difficult task for several reasons. First of all, the use of universal symbols in the tarot—images commonly seen in medieval art—invites an endless variety of interpretations. But it is the same ambiguity of these universal symbols which allows for a greater element of disguise. Secondly, the fact that the images in the tarot were changed from time to time caused the meanings of the cards to change as well. What we must investigate is why such alterations were made and how the meanings of the cards were influenced by these changes.

In addition, in attempting to show a connection with the Cathar movement, we are faced with the fact that most of the actual Cathar writings are no longer available to us as the Church burned all heretical texts that were found. We know, however, that Cathar books existed. Robert, count of Montferrand, for example, was said to possess an entire library of Cathar literature, but he was eventually persuaded by Dominican priests to destroy it.[10] "Unfortunately for us," says Haskins, "the destruction of their heretical literature was carried out so thoroughly that the teachings of its authors are scarcely known outside of the citations and refutations of its enemies, [the inquisitors]".[11] And because of the reluctance on the part of condemned heretics to give up their faith, even under the threat of death, we may assume that they took many of their secrets with them. It is possible, however, that we might find a few clues in an exploration of the art of the time.

As we have mentioned, medieval art was largely religious in nature, most of it being commissioned by the Church. In this way, paintings and sculptures decorating church architecture served as religious text-books. As Bishop Guillaume Durand of Mende explained in 1296, "Pictures and ornaments are the lessons and scriptures of the laity."[12] Paintings and sculpture also offered lessons in history, philosophy, and the natural sciences. Morris Bishop explains that "all medieval painting and sculpture was what is now called literary. It was illustrative, descriptive, telling a story, sometimes in sequences like a comic strip."[13] We know that other religious groups also used this same visual form of education. For example, the Waldensians' another heretical sect of the twelfth century, were known to use allegorical illustrations in their teachings. In a similar way, the tarot may have been used as an instructional tool and not just as a card game. Stuart Kaplan, author of the three-volume *Encyclopedia of Tarot*, postulates that some of the early decks (such as the fifteenth century Tarocchi of Mantegna) "were intended simply as a source of instruction regarding certain philosophic doctrines or precepts of morality."[14]

In his book, *The Tarot*, Richard Cavendish agrees with this explanation of the use of the tarot and explains that "teaching became an important function of cards.... Many special packs of cards have been invented for educational purposes as well as, or instead of, amusement."[15] The sixteenth and seventeenth centuries saw playing cards made to teach logic and law, history and geography, along with lessons from the Bible. Cavendish continues his review of the history of the cards by writing that "from education to propaganda is a short step and many packs have been designed to promote political attitudes, satirize and caricature opponents, or teach partisan versions of history."[16] One might imagine, then, that politically incorrect conversation such as that found in heretical circles may have been camouflaged in the tarot to preserve its message and at the same time avoid conflict with authority. In some respects, this may be similar to the way some political dissension and satire was adapted in nursery rhymes. For example, "Jack and Jill" was written in reference to the beheading of King Louis XVI of France in 1793 and his queen, Marie Antoinette, whose head came "tumbling after." Other common nursery rhymes such as

"Humpty Dumpty" and "London Bridge Is Falling Down" have their own political and historical references.

An example of symbols in medieval art: The Emperor Henry VI receiving the symbols of Fortitude and Justice from the Virtues, with the Wheel of Fortune in the foreground crushing his rival, Tancred of Lecce. Reproduced by permission of Burgerbibliothek Bern, Cod. 120.II f. 146r.

We have already seen that some authors like Alfred Douglas have drawn a connection between the tarot and the Cathars. Several others have also suggested the idea that secret information belonging to heretical sects may have been associated with the tarot. As early as 1911, Arthur Edward Waite wrote, "One brilliant opportunity has at least been missed, for it has not so far occurred to any one that the tarot might perhaps have done duty and even originated as a secret symbolic language of the Albigensian sects."[17] However, both Douglas and Waite fail to identify the specific images in the cards associated with the Cathar heresy. Waite is inspired by the broader spiritual implications of the new cards he had designed as a member of the Order of the Golden Dawn, and Douglas limits his description of the cards to the philosophy of the Gnostic tradition—The Fool is "man's spirit ... imprisoned in a physical body"; the Chariot and the Lovers are "challenges of everyday existence"; Death is "the sublimation of the lower self"; Temperance is "spiritual energy," and so on. Unfortunately, any specific details or characters relating to the historical events of the Cathar saga are left out.

One important factor that needs to be addressed in making a claim of a Cathar-tarot connection is the element of time. After all, the transition between the vanquishing of the Cathars during the Albigensian Crusade and the creation of the Tarot of Marseilles is significant. The Tarot of Marseilles appears to be a product of the fifteenth century at the earliest and didn't reach its popularity until the sixteenth or seventeenth century, which places it several hundred years after the events of the Albigensian Crusade. Part of the problem with this argument, however, is that we really don't know for sure when the earliest tarot appeared in its Marseilles form, since many cards and templates were destroyed when found by Church representatives. Although the "official" Tarot of Marseilles sold today are copies of decks dating from the seventeenth and eighteenth centuries, we have evidence of cards with similar imagery from much earlier dates. Kaplan writes that it was "probably during the late 15th or early 16th century that the tarot of Marseilles first emerged as a type of deck."[18] Many of the images found in the Tarot of Marseilles closely resemble the early Italian decks of the fifteenth century. This suggests that the development of the Tarot of Marseilles was more likely an evolutionary process which stemmed from these Italian counterparts than the appearance of a completely new form of the cards.

On the other end of this timeline, records of the Inquisition show that heretics in France and Italy were still being prosecuted well into the fourteenth century. If we use the fifteenth century as the time of the development of the Tarot of Marseilles, this still places its existence within only a hundred years or so—only a few generations—from the actual Cathar persecutions taking place. It would not be difficult to imagine that vital information was being transferred orally during that time—a method commonly used to pass on important or secret knowledge. Furthermore, survivors of the Albigensian war became refugees in other areas, thereby having the opportunity to pass on their messages to others in those communities. O'Neill explains that "the Waldensians [another heretical group] still existed in the eighteenth and nineteenth century.... There may also be remnants of the Cathari still in existence.

Thus, there is considerable evidence that the dualistic heretical sects were still alive and well during the period that the tarot was being designed."[19]

In addition, as we have mentioned earlier, the Tarot of Marseilles may not have been created by the Cathars themselves, but by others living well after they had vanished from the area. These people, possibly descendents of the Cathar refugees of the Albigensian Crusade, could have concealed the story of their forefathers in the tarot's major arcana as a creative alternative to the oral transmission of these stories.

One might ask why the early Cathars of the thirteenth century didn't think of this themselves. The simple answer is that playing cards weren't around at that time. The earliest evidence of cards in Europe places them around the 1370's. So it would have been left to the faithful of the fifteenth century to discover a different use for this new game.

We should also consider the fact that after about one hundred years or so after the Albigensian Crusade, the threat of the Inquisition had died down considerably. This easing up of persecution may have allowed people to take actions or produce material that earlier would have been considered too risky. Therefore, it is reasonable to assume that Cathar religious information and the story of their violent oppression would have been taken up by sympathizers who, years later, found a way to hide their secrets in a new art form.

Regarding the likelihood of the Cathars' complete demise, there is the distinct possibility that some of them may have survived by adapting to other, more mainstream, religious groups. Although they would have had to modify their theological perspective in most instances, this would have allowed them the more important benefit of continuing to practice their spiritual lifestyle, which was shared by other sects. Cathars may have found their way into the monasteries of the fifteenth and sixteenth centuries, perhaps encouraging some of the newer, even radical, ways of thinking which persisted through the Renaissance and the Protestant Reformation of later years. In this way, the heresy of the thirteenth and fourteenth centuries may have reemerged under the guise of other religious groups that challenged the Church.

Fourteenth century theologians who spoke out against the Church, were followed by others like Martin Luther (1483-1546) and John Calvin (1509-1564). In the fifteenth century, when the tarot was being created, Renaissance humanists stimulated the growth of intellectualism and religious consciousness, emphasizing the power of mankind to affect its own destiny. The thought of personal salvation outside of the Roman Catholic Church was seen as more of a real option. By this time, the so-called heretical messages of the tarot may have become more acceptable to the general public, contributing to its popularity. The disunity of religious doctrine and the variety of religious choices at the time may have been reflected earlier in the popular statement given to an inquisitor, "Just as there are seventy-two tongues, there are seventy-two faiths."[20]

The main point to be made regarding the preservation of the Cathars' story and spiritual tenets is that the succeeding generations of family members and close sympathizers, unwilling to lose the legacy of their forefathers, would have found a way to ensure that these messages were passed on. We should not assume that even the death of all the Cathars in Languedoc could have eradicated the entire set of teachings which remained with those who fled to safety. The loss of one family member didn't remove the sentiments of the other surviving members. The Inquisitor, Jaques Fornier, was told that when heresy entered into a home, "it was like leprosy and entrenched itself there for four generations or forever."[21] As this legacy became part of a family's or a community's heritage, it was not easily forgotten. And so the spirit which remained may have found its way into the tarot.

Let's consider a historical analogy: Let's suppose that the Germans had won World War II. Like all victors, they would have written—or rewritten—history from their perspective and to their advantage. Having control of the media, they might have produced films depicting themselves as the good guys, while showing the Jews and the allied forces as the bad guys. They might have published new history books for schools with their own information and outlawed other "inappropriate" reading material. Any practice of the Jewish religion would have been punishable by death, and anyone found giving aid to a Jewish family could also have been punished or put in jail.

As in real life in the 1930s and 1940s, to be a Jew would now be perilous. Your options would be few. If you had watched your friends and family being hauled off to the death-camps, you might either try to escape from Germany into a less dangerous country, or at least attempt to hide your real identity. The survival and the legacy of your religious traditions—and the real story of what happened to the Jews of Europe—might depend on your ability to communicate this information to others. But any attempt at openly discussing or writing about it could be disastrous if you were discovered by Nazi officials.

> *As a Jew, your best choice might be to find a way of hiding your traditions in a way that would not be easily detected. What would be better than to use something like tarot cards, which are already being openly used as a game in society? Because of the universality of the images, the commonly accepted meanings of the cards could afford safety. It also wouldn't be that difficult to introduce new, secret meanings for the cards. In fact, you might create a new style of cards with images that better suit your messages. Those who were taught to read these images could pass on the spiritual teachings of Judaism and the history of the Holocaust to future generations.*
>
> *It is quite possible that a similar situation inspired the Cathars of the Middle Ages, or those sympathizers who followed, to act in a similar manner.*

In order to create a secret method of instruction, it is not necessary to invent an entirely new form of art. It is evident that the Tarot of Marseilles borrowed images which were common to medieval art. That most of these images are derived from other sources is not in question. In fact, this is how most medieval artists worked—by reproducing themes already in use. Therefore, it is not surprising to find associations with a variety of medieval sources in the tarot system, such as the zodiac, the stages of man's life, the virtues, figures of the social order, or the astrological bodies. In fact, the similarities to traditional images convinced some historians to inadvertently consign the tarot to a number of questionable sources. Gertrude Moakley, for example, proposed that the entire pack of tarot cards was inspired by the figures of the renaissance procession as depicted in

Petrarch's *I Trionfi* due to some similarities between the two. Huson follows a similar line of reasoning and suggests that the tarot trumps were derived from the images of the popular "dance of death" motif of the Middle Ages and from medieval mystery plays, which depicted Christian themes of Jesus' life, crucifixion, and resurrection. In Italy, these plays were staged on wagons referred to as *trionfi*, which were carried from town to town.[22] The basic problem with these two theories is that they do not offer a complete explanation of the tarot—each author provides an association with some, but not all of the cards. In addition, the images of Jesus, essential to the mystery plays are clearly missing from the tarot. Instead, we find somewhat heretical themes. As O'Neill explains, "The images on the cards are taken from the art of the period. But this does not imply that the designers intended to symbolize precisely the same thing as the original artists."[23] And Gurevich explains that in "the endless repetitions, in the variations on the same theme and in the handling of standard concepts and images, medieval man found confirmation of his beliefs."[24] In a similar fashion, the tarot found a way to create its own distinct and radical messages through the commonly used images of the time.

In the case of the Tarot of Marseilles, some cards maintained a similarity to earlier decks and, when the purpose required changes, some images were borrowed from other sources. What we must ask ourselves is whether the creators of the Tarot of Marseilles had specific intentions in mind when making these changes or whether we feel comfortable dismissing these differences as random acts of artistic license, or even to the artist's misunderstanding of the original art they were copying. What is clear is that the tarot took on a significantly unique look when it began to be manufactured in a new region. These changes to the tarot reflected the need for a new set of symbols to reflect a new meaning—one that could not entirely be presented with the symbolism of the existing images.

In order to really understand the new design, some basic questions need to be asked. Why were some of the cards in the Tarot of Marseilles altered from those of the earlier decks in the first place? Why were certain images added while others were deleted? What was the purpose, for example, of adding a third person to The Lovers, or placing barking dogs in The Moon? What was the significance of placing two children in The Sun, or introducing The Tower to the deck? Why is the image of Death depicted in a way that differs from earlier sources? Are these just the arbitrary, creative flights of imagination, or was there another, more intentional, reason for using these particular images and making these specific changes?

As Cynthia Giles has written, "Little is known of how and why certain changes were introduced into the Marseilles images, but one possibility is that among the guilds of card makers who produced the many popular Tarot decks of the Marseilles period were members of heretical religious sects or secret societies who added their own symbolism to the design of the cards."[25] Again, although we are met with another author who has brought this important connection to our attention, we are left without a clear identification of what those symbols mean or what they refer to. This book goes beyond the identification of the connection between the tarot and its heretical source and attempts to interpret the actual images of the cards within this context.

Due to the scarcity of accurate and unbiased references, plus the simple fact that communication of ideas can change in six hundred years, any interpretation of the tarot will naturally be less than perfect. The fact that the real meaning of the cards was never written down makes it impossible to recreate a fully accurate "reading" as it was originally intended. There are some images on the cards whose true meanings may be lost through time and culture. In addition, due to the intentional secrecy involved, the element of disguise can make the interpretation of these hidden meanings understandably difficult. Therefore, we may never fully grasp the original messages of the cards in their entirety. What is important to discover, is whether a preponderance of the evidence will provide enough support for us to reach a reasonable conclusion as to their content and voice.

In Part II of this book, the tarot cards are described within their historical perspective. The process first requires establishing the association of each card in the context of our story. Some of the cards may have several meanings, references, or levels of interpretation. Each card may represent a historical person or event, and ideal or a spiritual lesson—or a combination of these. In some cases, more than one person might be associated with a specific card. In many cases, the cards have both historical and spiritual meanings. The Sun, for example, has a historical reference as well as an astrological and spiritual message. Because of this, the tarot can be "read" differently and interpreted on several levels, perhaps in accordance with the understanding of the audience or the intention of the reader.

Of course, any interpretation of the tarot will involve a measure of imagination as well as a search for evidence. The "rules of the game" never included a description of the meaning of the cards. So, even if one is accurate as to the true intentions of the creators of the tarot and places it in its proper context, a degree of interpretive license is still required to explain the images being presented.

But before we proceed to the cards, it is important to take a brief look at the historical environment, significant events, major characters, and spiritual teachings which found their way into the Tarot of Marseilles. In this way, we can establish a reference from which to base our understanding of the secrets in the cards.

PART ONE

—

The History

The Church

∾

The corruption of the people has its chief sources in the clergy.

—Pope Innocent III
Address to the Fourth Lateran Council, 1215

By the first millennium, Europe was basically a collection of Christian nations. One estimate is that there was about one church for every two hundred people.[26] The Roman Catholic Church had emerged as the most powerful center of influence, holding large tracts of land, bringing in a substantial income from its mandatory tithes, and establishing itself as the continent's spiritual police. Unfortunately, along with power and control came the abuses and corruption we commonly see in other political organizations throughout history. The condition of the Church in the Middle Ages inspired the famous medieval poet, Francesco Petrarca, or Petrarch (1304-1374), to write, "The wondrous temple built by Jesus Christ, once the invincible fortress against enemies of holy religion, has now in our times become a den of heartless thieves."[27] One of the greatest writers to emerge from the Middle Ages was undoubtedly Dante Alighieri (1265-1321). In his famous *Divine Comedy*, an allegorical characterization of life at the time, he assigned the innermost circles of hell to the kings, popes and high priests whom he felt deserved the severest punishment for their abuse of the trust placed in them. It's not hard to see why he felt so cynical toward those holding religious power.

From the beginning of its development, Christianity was challenged by its splintering of groups, each with diverse and often conflicting beliefs. During its evolution after Jesus walked the earth, followers of the apostles and other religious leaders—often separated by vast geographical distances and different languages—formed separate organizations which had their own interpretations of what it meant to be Christian. There was not just one official Church, nor had there always been one pope or one Bible. These later developments occurred only as a form of natural selection. While an orthodox church was attempting to claim its position as the head of Christianity, other factions—many of them Gnostic—were competing for their own converts, and many other "gospels" were being circulated. As early as the second century, church leaders such as Origen and Irenaeus were already attacking the writings of heretics who maintained radically different views from their orthodox position.

At that time, the Christian population was broadly divided between the West (which believed in the literal story of Jesus, along with the crucifixion and the resurrection), and the East (in which the "inner mysteries" were more important than one's faith in the historical Jesus). It was the western literalists who developed into the Catholic Church of Rome and eventually gained dominance over the other groups. Much of this shift occurred when the Emperor Constantine converted to Christianity in the fourth century. Constantine made a concerted effort—often by threat of death or banishment—to force his subjects to adopt the new religion. But even with large numbers of people choosing to convert, an official Christian doctrine had not been agreed upon. Inconsistencies within the gospels and other religious writings were often fuel for debate, and no single way of practicing Christianity was universally accepted at the time. To address this problem, Constantine called the Council of Nicea in 325 so that Church leaders could decide what would be official policy and what would, by exclusion, be classified as heresy. Those declared to be heretics were excommunicated and even put to death. Evidence of the Church's policy of intolerance toward those who didn't accept the official party line soon became clear. For example, one Christian leader, Arius, disagreed with the Church's interpretation of Jesus as God. Because of this, over three thousand of his followers were killed. Over the next several hundred years, other groups with divergent ideas found themselves in constant risk of a similar fate.

By the Middle Ages, the bishop of Rome had become the most powerful leader in the Christian world and, in all practicality, had a part in every aspect of life, from first communion to last rites. The Roman Catholic Church was now the official spiritual power on earth and the local bishop became the necessary intermediary between man and God. "His bestowal or withholding of the sacraments decided the fate of immoral souls."[28] Basically, this meant that if you were not baptized, you were not going to heaven. "What the Church offered was salvation, which could be reached only through the rituals of the established Church and by permission and aid of its ordained priests. '*Extra ecclesian nulla sala*' (No salvation outside the Church) was the rule."[29]   On the community level, no self-respecting city could claim real power without a local bishop. Even kings were subject to the sanction of Rome, crowned with the approval of the pope and occasionally excommunicated for disobedience. One of the primary sworn duties of a European king was to uphold the policies of the Church and to destroy heresy wherever it was found, for heresy was seen as the worst of all sins and therefore deserving of the most severe punishment.

At the turn of the first millennium, many people began to question the policies of the Church. One of the major causes of discord during this time concerned the Church's wealth and power. It didn't help the Church's cause when simple parishioners were confronted with the bishop's luxurious lifestyle, often accompanied by a reputation of greed, corruption, and debauchery. In her book, *The Medieval Vision*, Carolly Erickson writes, "Throughout western Europe the wealth of the church overshadowed even that of the secular nobility; this was to many sufficient proof that the church of Rome could not be the bearer of the true faith, since the true Christians had always been poor as well as oppressed."[30] In contrast to most of the heretical preachers who renounced wealth and material possessions, the Church took pride in its quest for wealth. An inscription over the door of the twelfth century church of St. Renis sums up this philosophy: "The soul on its earthly pilgrimage rises by material things to contemplate the Divine."[31] In his three-volume *History of the Inquisition of the Middle Ages*, Henry Lea offers this observation on the medieval Church: "In wise and devout hands, it might elevate incalculably the moral and material standards of European civilization; in the hands of the selfish and depraved it could become the instrument of minute and all-pervading oppression, driving whole nations to despair."[32]

Abuses were rampant. The construction of lavish churches was carried out to the financial detriment of the peasantry. Bishoprics were often sold to the highest bidders, as men seeking power and wealth saw these positions as a way to satisfy their greed. Other abuses included the enforcement of tithes, fines procured from confession, and the demand of fees for baptism, marriage, and death, often levied on impoverished villagers who could hardly afford them. "In too many cases," Lea explains, "the abbeys thus became centres of corruption and disturbance, the nunneries scarce better than houses of prostitution, and the monasteries feudal castles where the monks lived riotously and waged war upon their neighbors as ferociously as the turbulent barons."[33] The accumulation of money by the Church created a vast amount of land and income for itself, amounting to about three quarters of all wealth in France by the year 1500.

The pope in Rome was still the official head of the Church, but the corrupt state of the clergy was causing many people to seek religion elsewhere. In Languedoc, many found their answer in Catharism. The unfortunate state of affairs of the Church may have been part of why heretical groups like the Cathars grew in number during the twelfth century. However, along with the reaction to the internal abuses of the Church, this rise in dissent was also due to the Church's inability to satisfy the spiritual and intellectual needs of its flock. "Nowhere in Europe had culture and luxury made such progress as in the south of France," and yet, "nowhere in Europe ... were the clergy more negligent of their duties or more despised by the people."[34] The popularity of Catharism, then, was likely a product of several factors: the greater appeal of its message, the abuses of the Roman Catholic Church, and (perhaps just as important) the acceptance from many of the local aristocracy. In Languedoc, the counts of Foix, Narbonne, and Toulouse, for example, were all known supporters of the Cathars.

It is important to note that the retelling of the atrocities of the Albigensian crusade and the subsequent actions of the Inquisition are not meant to be an indictment of the Catholic Church. Indeed, despite episodes throughout history which it may not be proud of, Christianity has served as a moral inspiration and guidepost for numerous millions of people worldwide. However, regardless of their noble intentions or efforts to return wayward souls to spiritual life, the leaders of Christianity must, in the end, accept responsibility for what has occurred under its efforts—both good and bad.

Medieval Languedoc and the Counts of Toulouse

❦

There would have been no one in the world strong enough to rob me of my country if the Church had not existed.[35]

—Inscription on the tomb of Raymond VI

The thirteenth century was an era of change. It was the age of Dante and Petrarch, of Thomas Aquinas and Francis of Assisi. Marco Polo traveled along the Silk Road to China. King John of England signed the Magna Carta. Genghis Kahn was invading territories to the west of China and Christian soldiers were returning to Europe from the fourth crusade to the Holy Land. Most education, for those fortunate enough to afford it, was found within the monasteries where independent thought and scientific inquiry were generally discouraged and unauthorized books were banned. The University of Paris was first established in 1170, but as late as 1215, its faculty of arts forbade any discussion of the works of Aristotle. For most, there was no search for knowledge, as the Church provided all the acceptable answers. Any alternative views had to survive underground.

Society in medieval Europe was divided into three classes: nobles, merchants, and farmers (or serfs). The nobles were the landowners and allowed the farmers (who made up the largest of the three groups) to work their fields in exchange for protection, while the middle-class merchants conducted the trading of goods and services. Wealth and power were controlled by a select few. These feudal lords were in constant struggle with one another over territory and power, making war an almost constant part of life. For this reason, marriages in aristocratic families were often arranged for the purpose of creating alliances to reduce the threat of attack from their neighbors and to secure the wealth of ones estate. While the nobles were planning their wars and negotiating their truces, the majority of the people were concerned with the natural hazards of life: famine, flood, disease, and the threat of eternal damnation—for the Church still wielded the most power on all levels of life. To the three classes described earlier, then, the church and its clergy could be considered the fourth "leg" of the medieval table of life, offering stability in an uncertain world.

In the area of southern France which was then called Languedoc—named after the language of *oc* spoken there—many inhabitants were being converted to Catharism. This created a conflict between the Roman Church and the heretics it claimed were challenging its authority. Since one of the centers of Cathar heresy was the town of Albi, the southerners were sometimes referred to as Albigensians. In 1209, the wrath of the pope reached a climax when his call for a crusade was launched. The Albigensian Crusade pitted the Christians of northern France against their countrymen to the south and brought the horror of crusading to the European homeland. Although the declared purpose of the campaign was to fight heresy, many people in Languedoc were killed simply for attempting to protect their lands and homes. It also became clear that the central target of the crusade was Count Raymond VI of Toulouse.

Languedoc was a land which, in all practicality, was governed by an array of independent nobles. Toulouse, the largest city in Languedoc, was the major center of cultural and intellectual exchange at the time. It was the birthplace of the troubadour and of courtly love. By the thirteenth century, it had become a modern urban republic of sorts, where a growing middle class owned property and enjoyed the rewards of private business. As a result of the earlier crusades to the Holy Land, many men prospered from an increase in trade routes and new products from the East. The lower-class serfs were sometimes able to buy their freedom, something which offered a degree of hope for economic improvement to many families in the countryside. Citizens of Toulouse found a sense of independence and a tolerance of religion not found in other parts of Europe. Even Jews were allowed to hold public office, something that was not permitted in other areas of the country. Although the count of Toulouse was the head authority, the city had its own council made up of notable townsmen. This helped promote a degree of self-government and offered a form of progress from the traditional feudal system. In many ways, then, Toulouse represented the height of the modern European city. But during the Albigensian Crusade, it became the bastion of resistance. Often, the cry of "Toulouse" would be heard by soldiers racing across the battlefield or defending their homes.

View of Toulouse, circa 1650. Reproduced with permission from the Bibliotheque nationale de France.

The original lords of Toulouse had been the administrators for the Merovingian kings. The Merovingians, as readers of *Holy Blood, Holy Grail* may recall, were the keepers of the legend of how Mary Magdalene and her child (apparently the blood-line of Jesus) escaped the post-crucifixion turmoil of Jerusalem and landed in southern France. By the ninth century, the counts of Toulouse were in control not only of the city, but also many other parts of Languedoc. Count Raymond IV—one of the first leaders to take up the cross in the First Crusade to Jerusalem in 1096— was the ruler of no less than thirteen counties. During the time leading up to the Albigensian Crusade, the counts of Toulouse represented one of the most influential families in Languedoc. In the thirteenth century, Gervase of Tilbury described them as the "peers of kings, the superiors of dukes and counts."[36]

In 1195, at the age of thirty-eight, Raymond VI took over his family's territories, including the capital city of Toulouse, and became one of the most powerful rulers in Europe. Raymond's lands around Toulouse were almost as extensive as those of the French king in Paris, and although he was technically a vassal of Philip II of France, he acted with all the freedom and authority of an independent ruler.

Like most nobles of his day, Raymond saw marriage as an opportunity for political advantage. Having been married six times, he was related to many of Europe's most powerful royal houses—including those of Aragon, England, and France. He was the brother-in-law of King Peter of Aragon and also of Richard I of England. His mother, Lady Constance, was the daughter of Louis VI, and sister of Louis VII of France.

The seal of Count Raymond VI of Toulouse,
from the Archives Nationales de France.

It was clear from the beginning of the Albigensian Crusade that Raymond VI was being singled out as the major opponent in the Church's campaign against heresy in Languedoc. Raymond's reputation as a Cathar sympathiser was evident, if not by his direct support then by his tolerance, as is reflected in the *History of the Albigensian Crusade*, a chronicle written by the monk, Peter les Vaux-de-Cernay:

First it must be said that almost from the cradle he {Raymond}
always loved and cherished heretics, kept them in his domains and
honored them in whatever manner he could. Indeed, it is said that even
today, wherever he goes he takes with him heretics dressed as ordinary
people so that, when the time comes, he may die in their hands.[37]

This account of Raymond's sentiments was most likely
accurate, as he was said to have once pointed to a crippled
Cathar Perfect (or priest) and uttered, "I would rather be this
man than a king or an emperor."[38]

It was only after the pope's ambassador, Peter de Castelnau,
was murdered within Raymond's domain that Pope Innocent
III was able to stimulate a response to his call for a holy war
against heresy in the area. After Peter's murder, the count
was excommunicated and his ability to defend himself was
denied by the local church authorities. The personal attack on
Raymond was a key factor in the plan to crush the Albigensian
dissent. According to Peter les Vaux-de-Cernay, "If the Count
were allowed to prove his innocence [of his involvement in
Peter de Castelnau's murder], all the work of the Church would
be ruined."[39] In a desperate attempt to save himself and appease
the Church, Raymond finally vowed to purge his lands of all
heretics and agreed to suffer public humiliation by performing
penance in front of the church of St. Gilles. He joined the
crusaders temporarily and sent his only son, Raymond VII,
as hostage to Rome as a good faith offering. However, after it
became clear that nothing would satisfy the forces against him,
Raymond VI returned to Toulouse, and was welcomed as its

savior. His son also returned to help defend the city against the French crusaders.

Unfortunately for the young count, the northern forces eventually prevailed and he was forced to give in to the harsh demands of his adversaries. In 1229, Raymond VII signed the Treaty of Paris, which ended the Albigensian Crusade. In the end, he lost all his family's lands, including the major city of Toulouse and was left with only scraps of his once noble inheritance. This represented a huge takeover of an important family territory by a hostile force and created further animosity toward the Catholic Church.

Count Raymond VII takes an oath of allegiance to Louis IX at the Treaty of Paris in 1229. Reproduced with permission from the Bibliotheque nationale de France.

Although France ended its crusade against its neighbors to the south, the Church continued its pursuit of heresy through the establishment of the Inquisition. As we shall see, this had a profound impact on the life and religious expression of those living within the area. The fall of Toulouse and its noble family became, in a sense, a symbol of the loss of the Cathar and Albigensian resistance, but it may have also become a source of inspiration for the tarot.

The Cathars

∽

At Montmaur, Mirepoix, Laurac, and many other places
throughout the land, I saw heretics not only dwelling openly,
just like other men, but also openly preaching.... And truly,
nearly all men throughout the land would gather
together and go hear, and adore, the heretics.

—Guilhem de la Grassa
turn of the thirteenth century[40]

In 1177, Raymond V of Toulouse wrote a letter to Pope Alexander III concerning the spread of heresy in his land. The letter read, in part, as follows:

> *You know that in our region, the vineyards planted by the right hand of the Lord are destroyed by little foxes.... I plead with you therefore to rise up against them and make yourself like a wall of the house of Israel, lest their words, which spread like a cancer, become strong. So far has this stinking plague of heresy spread that nearly all who believe it think they are serving God ... priests are depraved ... churches lie vacant that once of old were venerated, baptism is denied... the resurrection of the flesh scornfully denied, and all the sacraments of the church refused, and—most sinful—they speak of two principles.... I find that my powers are inadequate to the task, for the more noble of my land are consumed with this heresy and with them a vast multitude of men, so that*

I dare not nor am I able to confront them.... Therefore, with a humble heart I run to seek your aid and counsel.... For this heresy is so deeply set in their entrails that it will not be destroyed without the strong hand of God....

Because we know that such heresy cannot be crushed by the power of the spiritual sword alone, it must also be punished with the corporeal sword. For this, I am convinced the king of France should be summoned; for I believe his presence will put an end to this evil. Should he come, I will open the cities to him ... show him the heretics, and—spilling blood, if that is what the business requires—help him wipe out the armies and enemies of Christ.[41]

This letter may have been written in response to the concerns of the pope, who was preoccupied with the fact that Catharism had become well established in Languedoc. In 1163, Pope Alexander III held a council at Tours in which he condemned heresy in Toulouse. In 1179, he denounced Catharism at the Third Lateran Council, noting that they were "thick on the ground in Gascony, the Albigeois, the Toulousain and elsewhere, and that they were poisoning the minds of ordinary people."[42]

Ironically, Raymond V's wishes to eliminate heresy from his province would prove disastrous to his heirs, who—some thirty years later—bore the full brunt of the forces of both France and Rome, when the Albigensian Crusade was unleashed on their domain. By then, tolerance toward heresy in Toulouse had shifted 180 degrees. The new count at that time was Raymond VI. Part of this change in sentiment may have been due to the sheer increase in the number of converts to Catharism, but it could also have been partly the result of the personal convictions of his second wife, Beatrice of Beziers. Beatrice was an enthusiastic supporter of the Cathars, and her affections may have had a significant influence on her husband during the thirteen years of their marriage. After their divorce, Beatrice actually became a Cathar Perfect herself.

The name *Cathari*, as they were called in Italy, is derived from the Greek word for "pure," which referred to their priests, who were called the *perfecti*, or Perfect. By the twelfth century, Catharism had become well established in Languedoc. Bernard of Clairvaux (later Saint Bernard)—possibly the most important voice of the Church at the time other than the pope—was sent to Toulouse in 1145 to preach against the rising heresy. It was said that without Bernard's preaching campaign, everyone there would have become a heretic within three years.[43] But even with the efforts of Bernard and other orthodox preachers, the presence of Catharism remained strong. Raimon du Fauga, bishop of Toulouse from 1232-1270, wrote, "For this city [Toulouse] and nearly all the countryside was at that time so wholly and catastrophically infected by the poison of the heresy that the Church of Jesus Christ seemed to perish in those places, and the Catholic faith to die, stifled beneath the brambles and thorns of perverse doctrines."[44] When asked why the heretics could not be expelled, a knight named Pons Adhemar, replied, "We cannot; we were brought up with them, there are many of our relatives amongst them, and we can see that their way of life is a virtuous one."[45]

At that time, open debate between heretics and Church representatives were common and held in public for all to hear. In 1165, for example, the bishop of Albi presided over an open religious debate between the Cathar Perfects and several leaders of the Roman Church, including the archbishop of Narbonne. Both sides used the New Testament, written in Latin, as support for their arguments, which indicates that the Cathar priests were as well versed in the Bible as their counterparts. Often, the conversion of those who were searching for spiritual answers was a matter hearing the right words delivered in these debates.

The growth of the Cathar presence in Languedoc seems to have occurred around the time of the first and second Crusades. It would seem likely that the French crusaders brought the dualist tradition of the East with them when they returned home from Constantinople. As we are told, "Numerous as the Cathars of Western Europe became, they always looked to the east of the Adriatic as to the headquarters of their sect."[46]

One major figure, Bishop Nicetas of Constantinople, sometimes referred to as Pope Nicetas or Papa, traveled from the Balkans through Italy to Languedoc to preside over a council at St. Felix in 1167. There, he spoke of religious matters and conferred the *consolamentum* (the Cathar ritual of baptism by the Holy Spirit) upon several Perfects, thus passing on the lineage from the Eastern Church to those in the west. Nicetas also helped to decide upon a major territorial division which split up the diocese of Languedoc into four bishoprics headed by the major families of Albi, Toulouse, Carcasonne, and Agen. (It wouldn't be surprising to discover that these four families were in fact those represented by the four suits of the tarot).

Much of the Cathar belief system brought to southern France by Nicetas was inherited from the Bogomils of tenth century Bulgaria. The Cathars shared many Bogomil customs, such as baptism by spirit, chastity, fasting, a prohibition against eating meat or dairy products, a dualistic philosophy (described below), and the denunciation of idols and symbols. (It is this last item which may explain why we do not see orthodox religious symbolism like the Christian cross in the tarot). The Bogomils, in turn, may have borrowed their ideas from other heretical groups going as far back as the Gnostics of the second century who believed in a dualistic universe and emphasized a personal spiritual "knowing" (*gnosis*), or awareness, between man and God.

In 1945, the famous Nag Hammadi scrolls were dug up in Egypt. Dating back to the earliest evangelists, these heretical writings, also known as the Gnostic Gospels, challenged much of orthodox Christianity. It is very possible that heretical groups preserved these Gnostic traditions—and possibly their texts—as Christianity continued to evolve. We are reminded that "from Bulgaria as well came preachers carrying New Testaments different from the Latin Vulgate, which the local Perfects translated into the vernacular."[47] Cathars were also known to have copies of apocryphal works such as the *Vision of Isaiah* and the *Book of St. John*.[48]

Surviving copies of these manuscripts allowed heretical sects to contemplate a different interpretation of the teachings of Jesus, which some thought reflected a more esoteric level of knowledge. Thus, in the Gospel of Mark, Jesus says to his disciples, "To you I teach these secret teachings, and to others they will hear them in parables" (Mark 4:12). Clement of Alexandria acknowledged that the gospels had been written in different versions, depending on the level of secrecy being divulged to initiates. In fact, it is believed that some of the "greater mysteries" were never written down. Thomas Gallus, a thirteenth century Franciscan (often called "the Frenchman"), wrote of the "two forms of knowledge of God," an intellectual one and another "incomparably better.... This superior wisdom is by way of the human heart."[49]

Many heretical sects, such as the Cathars, sought this esoteric approach which was more concerned with personal religious experience. They believed that a church was not needed for personal prayer, that anyone should be allowed to preach the gospels, and that the sacraments were invalid in the hands of immoral men. Thus, the role of the priest was challenged. Cathars also denied the traditional baptism by water and felt that infant baptism was useless, since the child would be too young to understand its meaning. The Cathars called their church the True Church or the Church of Love, and referred to the official Church of Rome as the False Church.

The primary Cathar ritual was the *consolamentum*, or baptism by spirit. It included the laying on of hands and the placing of a book (usually the Gospel of John) on the head of the initiate. The tradition of the "laying on of hands" was a common practice in the Eastern Orthodox Church and was believed to have actually been used by the followers of Christ. The Cathars felt that this tradition started with Jesus himself and was handed down from "the Good Men to the Good Men, until now."[50] Evidence of this practice can be found in the Bible: "Then Peter and John laid their hands on them and they received the Holy Spirit" (Acts 8:17).

Gnostics recognized at least three forms of baptism, that of water, fire and the Holy Spirit. The practice of the *consolamentum* may refer back to a higher baptism which Jesus acknowledged when he said to his apostles, "John baptized with water but ye shall be baptized with the Holy Ghost" (Acts 1:5). It was offered to the initiate after a long period of instruction. He was asked to pledge never again to sin, lie, take an oath, or harm any living thing. In addition, he was to refrain from sex, denounce worldly luxuries, and accept a diet free from animal products. However, because this lifestyle was so strict, only an elite group of Cathar Perfects actually chose to live according to its demands. Other Cathar supporters, called *credentes*, who made up the majority of converts, would usually accept the *consolamentum* on their death beds. In this way, it was performed more as a blessing or last rites to cleanse the sins of the believer and prepare him for the return of his soul to God. The ceremony concluded with the words, "May God bless you and make of you a Good Christian and bring you to a good end."[51]

St. Dominic confronts the Cathars. Reproduced with permission from the Bibliotheque nationale de France.

One of the fundamental principles which defined the Cathar heresy was their belief in dualism—a belief that dated back to Gnosticism and the early development of Christianity. Simply put, dualism answered the question of how an all-knowing, all-beneficent God could allow evil to exist. It solved this problem by claiming that there are actually two primary creative forces, one God who created spirit, which is good, and another god (Satan), who created the world of matter, which is evil. Man's dual nature was a combination of both. His God-given spirit was thought to be trapped in his material body until it was released upon death. This may help explain why so many Perfects seemed unafraid to die and went so willingly to the stake. The Cathar dualist philosophy is reflected in the words from their *consolamentum*: "Have no mercy on the flesh born in corruption, but have mercy on the spirit held in prison."[52]

Dualist philosophy contradicts the basic orthodox Christian creed, "We believe in *one* God, Father Almighty, creator of heaven and Earth" [italics added], and therefore became proof of heresy in and of itself.

Although the Cathars held on to philosophical heresies such as dualism, Wakefield tells us that "The heretics were not theologians, but simple people condemning a worldly priesthood out of a zeal for a purer evangelistic Christian life."[53] He adds, "It is probable that they won their first following in the West by their demonstration of piety and rigorous morality, which appealed so strongly to religious sentiments of the era, rather than because of their dualist theology."[54] In effect, although their dualistic beliefs may have provided evidence of heresy for the Church and the Inquisition, the average Cathar was less interested in theological concepts and more concerned with simply living a good life. They considered themselves Christians, living according to basic Christian values. Followers referred to the Perfects as the *boni homnis*, or the good men. Even St. Bernard of Clairvaux admitted of the Cathars, "No sermons are more Christian than theirs, and their morals are pure." Erickson reminds us that it would be wrong to assume that they were turning away from Christianity itself. "On the contrary," she says, "by rejecting the church it hoped to rediscover the pure core of biblical Christianity—the apostolic ideal—and to build a truer worship around it."[55] When asked what sort of men these Good Christians were, a Perfect named Guillaume Belibaste replied, "They are men like the others.... But they are the only ones to walk in the ways of justice and truth which the apostles followed."[56] As Wakefield writes, "None were humbler; none were more assiduous in prayer, more constant under persecution; none made more consistent claims to be 'good men'; and it was on those terms that they were received by many of the common people."[57]

It would seem, then, that the crime of heresy charged against the Cathars was one of doctrinal interpretation, and not by how they conducted their lives. And for this, they paid a steep price.

The Albigensian Crusade

∽

In the parts of Toulouse a damnable heresy has lately arisen, and like
a canker is slowly diffusing itself into the neighboring localities.

—from the fourth Canon of The Council of Tours, 1163

In 1095, Europe responded to the call of Pope Urban II to
reclaim the holy city of Jerusalem from Muslim control.
Although the first crusaders managed to capture Jerusalem in
1099, future campaigns were less successful. The Holy Land
was reclaimed a century later by Saladin and his armies, leaving
tens of thousands of men, women, and children slaughtered on
both sides of the conflict.

After nearly a hundred years of fighting, the enthusiasm
for the Crusades was waning. At first emboldened by their
participation in a holy war, believing they were protected by
divine providence, crusading armies were soon disillusioned by
their lack of success. It was about that time, late in the twelfth
century, that a closer enemy was found. Soon after his election in
1198, Pope Innocent III called for a crusade against the Cathar
heretics of Languedoc and upon those who supported them.

Innocent persistently sought the assistance of the French
monarchy for his new campaign. However, France was engaged
in its own political struggles against England and Germany
at the time. Then, in 1208, the pope found an excuse to

strengthen his case when his representative, Peter of Castelnau, was murdered in the district of Count Raymond VI of Toulouse. This was enough to stimulate a response from King Philip Augustus which sparked a crusade in 1209. The Albigensian Crusade lasted twenty years and was followed by almost one hundred years of further persecution by the Inquisition, which sought out heretics through a calculated policy of terror and intimidation. Although many of those convicted of heresy were simply jailed, sent on pilgrimages, or had their homes and possessions confiscated, thousands of others were tortured, burned, or otherwise executed. While the Cathars were drastically reduced in number, some survived, although not in the open fashion they had previously enjoyed.

Although Innocent's motives for initiating the Albigensian Crusade may have been religious in nature, it is doubtful that purging the southern counties of heresy was the primary objective of the French army. The opportunity to seize lands and possessions from wealthy families in Languedoc must have been a considerable incentive for the French king and his barons in the north, as Innocent had already set the rules of engagement by declaring that anyone could confiscate the lands of the heretics. In addition, the incentives provided to those willing to join the crusade for a mere forty days of service make one suspicious of their true motives. Along with the opportunity for gaining the spoils of war, those who volunteered were promised the usual indulgences such as the forgiveness of debts and the absolution of sins. In this way, the Crusade attracted many of the delinquent and criminal elements of society.

It has been said that with the initiation of the Albigensian Crusade, "Warfare in western Europe had reached a new level of horror, and all in the name of God."[58] The first wave of crusaders was an assembly of about 20,000 nobles, horsemen, and foot soldiers. Surviving records of eye-witnesses testify to the horrors inflicted on both sides. Men and women were burned alive. Heads, hands, and feet were lopped off and eyes were gouged out, partly to instill fear in others. In some cases, entire towns were wiped out, where all the inhabitants were put to death without question or regard to their religious faith.

Such was the case in 1209 in the town of Beziers, the first city to be attacked in the Albigensian Crusade and one which set the standard of violence for the rest of the campaign. Accounts tell us that a list of names of two hundred twenty potential heretics was presented to the bishop of Beziers by Arnold Amaury, the pope's officer in charge. These people were to be turned over to the crusading army if the rest wished to be spared. But the offer was rejected, and the town was besieged. When asked how they should differentiate between the heretics and the faithful, Amaury is said to have replied, "Kill them all. God will know his own." Whether he actually spoke these words or not, the results remain the same: approximately twenty thousand men, women, and children were indiscriminately put to the sword, including an estimated seven thousand who were massacred inside the Church of Mary Magdalene, where they had fled for sanctuary. After the massacre, Amaury wrote to the pope, boasting, "Our men spared no one, irrespective of rank, sex or age, and put to the sword almost 20,000 people. After this great slaughter the whole city was despoiled and burnt, as Divine vengeance raged marvelously."[59]

The Battle of Beziers. Reproduced with permission from the Bibliotheque nationale de France.

Other towns would fall, including Carcassonne, Lavaur, and Muret, where more civilians were killed and suspected heretics burned. A year after the massacre at Beziers, one hundred forty Cathars were burned alive at Minerve. Out of the ranks of the French troops, one man in particular rose to prominence and glory. His name was Simon de Montfort, Earl of Leicester. Montfort showed himself to be a natural leader of men, and his successes on the battlefield were chronicled in detail. Because of his early victories in the Albigensian Crusade, he obtained recognition from his peers as their champion. However, it soon became clear that his designs of personal gain overshadowed his dedication to the religious objectives of the campaign. In 1213, the pope sent Montfort a letter condemning his actions: "Not content with rising against the heretics, you have carried crusading arms against the Catholic population; you have spilt innocent blood, and have invaded ... the lands of ... the King's vassals, although the people of those lands were in no way suspected of heresy." Montfort was ordered to restore these lands "for fear that if you unjustly retain them it will be said that you have labored for your own advantage and not for the cause of the faith."[60]

But Montfort ignored the pope's letter and continued his pillaging. Despite his warning, the pope appointed Montfort as Lord of Languedoc and granted him vast amounts of land, including the county of Toulouse. The city of Toulouse remained under the leadership of Count Raymond VI, however, and would continue to be the greatest source of resistance to the crusaders. Montfort's attempts to conquer Toulouse were constantly thwarted, although he did succeed in taking over parts of the city for a short period of time. Montfort was eventually killed in battle when a stone hurled from a tower struck him in the helmet, crushing his head. (We will revisit Simon de Montfort when we look at The Chariot and Force in Part II).

After twenty years of war, King Philip Augustus of France decided to become more involved in the Albigensian conflict. Placing his war with England on hold and seeing an opportunity to seize taxable land in the south, he sent his son to lead an army against Raymond VII, who had by then taken over his father's title as Count of Toulouse. The count's attempts at obtaining support from his allies against the king failed, and he found himself in a desperate situation. Victory for the overwhelming French army was inevitable, and the young count finally surrendered to the crown in 1229 with the signing of the Treaty of Paris.

As part of the terms of the peace agreement, Raymond's daughter, Jeanne, was promised in marriage to one of the king's sons. Since Jeanne had no children of her own, the entire county of Toulouse transferred to the French crown upon her death, as Raymond had no other heirs. (We will come to this event again when we look at the images in The Sun). Thus, the legacy of the counts of Toulouse came to an end.

Although, technically, the Albigensian crusade was over, persecution of the Cathars continued. One of the major turning points in this struggle was the battle of Montsegur. The castle of Montsegur, in the county of Foix, was built high upon a hill surrounded by cliffs and served as a refuge for Perfects and *credentes* fleeing the destruction of their towns. During the long siege of Montsegur, Count Raymond VII dispatched messengers to the castle with promises that he would arrange for reinforcements to be sent from Frederick II, the Holy Roman Emperor. Unfortunately, this support never materialized, and after a long siege by the French, the forces at Montsegur were finally forced to surrender. During the negotiations of the terms of surrender, the Cathar leaders arranged for their treasures to be secretly removed from the castle by two men who were lowered down the cliffs. They were instructed to hide the treasure in nearby caves and to ensure that certain information would be preserved. Today, we can only speculate as to what this contained as we have no record of such a treasure ever being found.

Upon surrendering at Montsegur, the Cathars were given the choice of renouncing their faith or meeting their death. Almost everyone chose the latter. Over two hundred Cathars were burned in a massive pyre which was hastily built at the base of the castle. A monument erected in their memory can still be seen there today. The fall of Montsegur in 1244 was considered the blow that ultimately broke the back of the Cathar resistance. The conquerors wrote to the pope, "We have crushed the head of the dragon."[61]

The ruins of Montsegur Castle. Photo by Gerbil.

Heresy now had to survive in secrecy. To avoid detection by those who would turn them in to the Church authorities, the remaining Perfects were forced to live underground. Evidence tells us that groups of Cathars were still influential in various towns such as Montaillou, where they were discovered by the Inquisition as late as 1320.[62] Many Cathars fled to the mountains and to Italy (especially to Lombardy in northern Italy) to avoid the Inquisition. There they may have found shelter in other religious groups, such as *Humiliati* or the *Pateria*, both popular religious organizations which shared many values with Catharism. In addition, the fleeing Cathars may have been offered protection by powerful families, such as the Visconti of Milan, who had no love for the pope. It would seem reasonable to assume that elements of Cathar sympathies were found in the origins of the Italian tarot, where it was born.

Evidence of Cathar flight to Italy is clear. As early as 1229, Charles of Anjou sent letters to all nobles and magistrates in the area, instructing them that "the inquisitors of France were about coming or sending agents to track and seize the fugitive heretics who had sought refuge in Italy."[63] And from records of the Inquisition, we know that two hundred heretics were burned in the arena at Verona in 1278.[64] The flight of Cathar refugees to Italy from the Albigensian war was a natural event. Languedoc and northern Italy had long shared both economic and religious ties. They enjoyed common trade routes and Cathar communities had already been established there. In fact, Cathar communities were known to exist in Italian cities as early as 1160.[65] The inquisitor, Anselm of Alessandria, spoke of Cathar bishoporics in northern Italy in the 1260's and Cathars were known to have had their own schools in cities like Verona and Milan at the beginning of the thirteenth century.[66] Many Italian families, referred to as Ghibellines, were opponents of the pope and would have offered protection for the Cathar fugitives. The case of Oberto Pallavicini offers evidence of this. Pallavicini was a wealthy noble who controlled several territories in northern Italy. As part of his trade agreements, he issued a toll to be paid by all who passed through his land in exchange for protection from theft. However, this excluded anyone traveling on foot with a simple bundle on his back, who paid nothing. This would have made it easy for fugitives from Languedoc to move through the area undisturbed. In 1260, Pope Alexander IV issued a decree against Pallavicini, accusing him of heretical sympathies and alleging that he was harboring fugitives.

Heretics were also known to have fled to the outskirts of Languedoc, and some remained in cities and rural areas. In 1250 there were still at least two hundred known Perfects in the city of Toulouse. Given the deep religious convictions of the Cathars and the degree to which they were interwoven in the communities, it would not have been easy for the Church to eradicate them completely from the area. More evidence exists that some Cathars fled to other parts of Europe as well. In 1325, Pope John XXII complained that "a great crowd of heretics gathered together from many different regions has flocked to the principality of Bosnia."[67]

It may also be possible that some surviving heretics, after going underground, resurfaced at a later time and reinvented themselves under another guise. Some, for example, may have found sanctuary in the monasteries of the Spiritual Franciscans, who were regarded as radicals by the Church. By the mid-thirteenth century, the Franciscan order was divided into two factions. One followed the papacy, whereas the other, called the Spirituals, followed St. Francis' original teachings of poverty. The Spirituals had their share of disagreements with the Church in Rome. The Franciscan Raymond Garsias spoke out against the corruption of the Church and called all the crusaders "murderers," and in 1319, four Spirituals were burned as heretics in Marseilles. The Beguins, who called themselves the Poor of Christ, were another monastic group who branched off from the Franciscan order in the early fourteenth century and may have provided shelter for remaining Cathars. The Beguins consisted mainly of women, and as such, may have offered an opportunity for Cathar women to find a new home away from the threat of the relentless inquisitors.

It is not being suggested that these groups shared all of the same religious beliefs of the Cathars, but their lifestyle of piety and poverty and the legitimacy of their order may have offered Cathar refugees the sanctuary they needed. As Wakefield explains, "In the fourteenth and fifteenth centuries doctrinal criticism, spiritual discontent, and extravagant or unorthodox expressions of piety would continue to appear, in old and new forms."[68] Bernard Gui, who was commissioned by Pope Clement V as an inquisitor in the diocese of Toulouse from 1307 to 1324, wrote a treatise on how to interrogate heretics in which he points out, "Also, in order to protect themselves, they sometimes push themselves into feigned familiarity with members of religious orders and the clergy ... thus to acquire for themselves and theirs a freer opportunity to remain undiscovered."[69]

Although one might question such a theory, suggesting that the Cathars' unwavering faith would prevent them from living under the rule of other religious orders, we must keep in mind that Cathars may have been compelled to choose this option to insure their very existence in these desperate times. We should also keep in mind that the Cathars themselves were not always united under one central theology. When Nicetas was summoned from the East to bring order to Languedoc, the Cathars were already divided into at least six dioceses, each with their own individual differences. In the first place, there were disagreements regarding the correct form of dualism—a difference revolving around whether there was originally only one God who then created Satan (mitigated dualism), or two gods from the very beginning, one good and one evil (absolute dualism). In addition, arguments arose concerning the body of Christ, the existence of free will, and the acceptance of miracles.[70] By the time the Cathars had migrated into Italy from Languedoc, these differences became more apparent as teachings were modified according to the understanding of their leaders. Rainerius Sacconi, a converted Cathar who became a Dominican friar, wrote in 1250 that the Cathars are "divided into three parts or principal groups, the first of which is called the Albanenses, the second the Concorezzenses, the third the Bognolenses.... All the Cathars have general beliefs in which they agree and particular ones in which they differ."[71]

It's difficult to know when the last Cathars lived, since we only have records of those who were caught and prosecuted. And it's unlikely that surviving Perfects would have advertised their whereabouts. On the contrary, they found ways of hiding and protecting themselves during a time of persecution, often creating secret signals to avoid detection. For example, when a believer entered a strange house, he would say, "Is there a crooked stick here?" The answer may be "be seated," indicating that there was no one there to fear.[72]

Many groups of Cathars survived into the fourteenth century. It was recorded in the Book of the Inquisition of Toulouse that 636 "culprits" were sentenced between 1308 and 1323.

Rene Weiss gives a vivid account of some of the last known Cathars in *The Yellow Cross*. One man in particular, Peter Auteri, became a well known Perfect along with his brother in an area around Toulouse. Like many of the religious converts before him, Peter gave up a good career and sold his possessions to follow the Cathar faith. He was often found traveling through towns like Montailou—almost all of whose inhabitants were known to be Cathars. As late as 1305, Auteri was holding services at the Church of St. Cross in Toulouse and ordaining other Cathar ministers. After years of evading his persecutors, he was finally captured in 1311. His last words, as he was taken from prison to be burnt at the stake, were, "If I had been allowed to preach to you, you would all have embraced my Faith."[73] The last recorded Cathar lived in Florence in 1342, well over a hundred years after the end of the Albigensian Crusade. But as one author has suggested, "communities lingered on later still."[74]

In the year 1203, a priest named Dominic de Guzman accompanied Bishop Diego of Osma on a mission from Spain to Denmark where they encountered the Cathars on their way through southern France. Dominic later returned to the area to preach against heresy and, with a grant from Bishop Fulk, established the first house of preachers in Toulouse. Dominic realized that the impression being made by the Church was counterproductive. Upon meeting the pope, he reported on the state of affairs in Toulouse: "It is not by the display of power and pomp ... that the heretics win converts; it is ... by seeming holiness." Thus, he attempted to use the Cathars' own methods by preaching poverty and humility. In 1216, Innocent III responded by granting Dominic permission to found the Order of Preaching Friars, better known as the Dominicans.

Dominic died in 1221, but the order he founded was to become the chief instrument of the Inquisition—an organization which was to leave its mark on the population for generations to come. As Thomas Cahill puts it, "Dominic had founded his order not as a model of evangelical poverty but as an assault engine."[75] In a play on words, *Dominicanus* (Dominicans) becomes *Domini canes*, or the Lord's hounds (something we will encounter later when we look at The Fool). Of the Inquisition, Henry Lea writes, "Human wickedness and folly have erected, in the world's history, more violent despotisms, but never one more cruel, more benumbing, or more all-pervasive."[76] Beginning in the 1230s, Dominican inquisitors brought fear into every town they visited, and abuses of power became commonplace. Many families were devastated, like the Mirepoix-Pereille clan, which had at least thirty-three known Perfects, ten of whom were burned at the stake. At times, the bodies of deceased heretics were exhumed, dragged through the streets, and burned again while heralds shouted, "Who behaves thus shall perish thus."[77]

The influence of the Inquisition was felt at every level of society. Every citizen was expected to aid the local inquisitors in their search for heretics, and reluctance to do so placed one under suspicion. Every adult was obligated to appear before the bishop three times a year to confirm his or her loyalty to the orthodox faith. In 1234, a council in Beziers gave permission to anyone to accuse anyone else and have them arrested for heresy.[78] The accused would then have to prove their innocence or receive their punishment.

"Heretics of all sorts were outlawed," Lea writes, "and when condemned as such by the Church they were to be delivered to the secular arm to be burned. If, through fear of death, they recanted, they were to be thrust in prison for life, there to perform penance. If they relapsed into error, thus showing that their conviction had been fictitious, they were to be put to death. All the property of the heretic was confiscated and his heirs disinherited.... Those who defended the errors of heretics were to be treated as heretics.... All rulers and magistrates, present or future, were required to swear to exterminate with their utmost ability all whom the Church might designate as heretics, under pain of forfeiture of office."[79] In fact, the success of the Inquisition may have been rooted in the extent to which they made the choice of heresy intolerable.

"Condemned at the Stake." Reproduced with permission from the Bibliotheque nationale de France.

In 1235, outraged citizens of Toulouse finally threw the Dominicans out of town, although they were later reinstated. While the efficiency of the Inquisition's tactics is unquestioned, the fact remains that an unknown number of heretics did survive. In the first quarter of the fourteenth century—almost a hundred years after the arrival of the Inquisition—hundreds of people were still being accused of heresy and many more had fled as fugitives.

It is not hard to see how the impact of the Albigensian war and the subsequent actions of the Inquisition had left deep wounds not soon to be forgotten. The desperation of the surviving heretics and the anger of local citizens are reflected by the words of Peter Garcias of Toulouse, who was recorded to have said to a Franciscan friar, "If I get my hands on this God who created so many souls to save but a few and damn all the rest, I'd rip him apart with my fingernails and my teeth." Regarding the Church of Rome, he added, "An official who judges someone a heretic and has them put to death is a murderer.... The preachers of crusades are criminals."[80] With so much anger and memory of a brutal past, some may have been encouraged to find a way—secretive and disguised from the Church's watchful eyes—to preserve their history and religion for future generations. The development of the Tarot of Marseilles may have supplied just such a method.

In the case of the Albigensian Crusade, the spoils of war went to the King of France and to Rome. If the Cathars had been left alone, it's very likely that they would have continued to flourish in Languedoc, and their heresy may have become the dominant religion of the area. They practiced their understanding of Christianity as it had been passed down to them through the centuries. However, their sins of heresy were punished with unforgiving brutality. Given the evidence at hand, it's not difficult to see how the Cathars viewed the world as evil, in the clutches of the devil. To the medieval Church, the greatest sin was heresy; to the Cathars, it was vanity. History has given us ample evidence of the faults of the latter.

The Development of the Tarot

❧

It would be fascinating to identify the emotion or circumstance intended by each card. Some personages and scenes on the cards were probably drawn from actual people and events from the times, but the precise history represented by the cards remains a mystery.

—Stewart R. Kaplan, *The Encyclopedia of Tarot,* Vol. II[81]

As far as we know, playing cards were introduced into Europe around the 1370's, most likely from Arabic sources. At that time, the typical deck consisted of just the four suits—cups, swords, batons, and coins. The addition of the twenty-two "triumphs," which are commonly referred to as the major arcana, probably appeared in the early 1400s, and commonly define the tarot as a new form of cards. Hand-painted tarot cards have survived from that era which were made for aristocratic Italian families and Charles VI of France. In 1450, Francisco Sforza wrote a letter requesting several packs of "triumph" cards, which tells us that the cards were available for purchase at least by that time. Records from 1442 of the D'Este family court at Ferrara also refer to a pack of *tarocchi* cards. The word "tarot" is a French adaptation of the Italian *tarocchi,* which was derived from the earlier Italian *trionfi*, or "triumph" (from which we get our "trumps").

Curiously, nobody really knows why the picture cards, or trumps, were added to the deck of regular playing cards, or why the creators of those cards chose the specific images they did. And because most of the decks were lost or destroyed, we are unfortunately left with only a small sampling of what was likely produced. Regardless of the real reason they were developed, it would seem unlikely that an entire set of twenty two images was created simply to add another dimension to a trick-taking card game already in existence.

Many authors place the official introduction of the Tarot of Marseilles in the seventeenth century. However, decks with similar images existed much earlier, making the date of its first appearance a bit speculative. One of the earliest forms of tarot cards similar to the Marseilles style is found in what we call the Cary-Yale sheet, which is an uncut sheet of tarot images housed in the Beinecke Rare Book Manuscript Library at Yale University. It dates from the 1500s and was probably produced in Milan. During this time, Milan was ruled by the Visconti-Sforza family, whose members were huge patrons of the arts and employed some of the greatest names of the time, including Leonardo da Vinci and Francesco Petrarca, sometimes referred to as the Father of Renaissance Humanism. From the fourteenth through the mid-sixteenth century, Milan, the capital of Lombardy, was (perhaps not coincidentally) known as both a card-making district and a center of heresy. It may have been in the cities of Milan and Ferrara where the heretical qualities of the tarot began to find their place through the support of sympathetic patrons like the Visconti and D'Este families, both of whom were openly opposed to the papacy in Rome. In 1321, for example, Pope John XXII accused Matteo Visconti of heresy and sorcery, and in 1435, Pope Eugenius IV even hired an assassin to have Francesco Sforza killed. There are also similarities between the Visconti-Sforza family of Milan and Raymond VI of Toulouse. Both fought against the papacy and faced threats of excommunication. Both fought against the French crown. Both had family ties through marriage to England, France and Spain. And both were political allies of the Holy Roman Emperor.

The Cary-Yale tarot sheet. Beinecke Rare Book and Manuscript Library, Yale University.

What appears to be the most accepted theory of the origins of the tarot, complete with its major arcana, was that it was a product of medieval Italy. After twenty years of research, Robert O'Neill reached the conclusion that "individual images or subsets of the symbolic system can be found in other places, but the totality of the symbolic system [of the tarot] is only found in 15th century Italy."[82] Why certain symbols and images were chosen, however, remains a mystery.

There is speculation that the tarot was brought into France following the French conquest of Milan in 1494-1498. At this time, the growth and popularity of the tarot in France was likely due to the support of new patrons who commissioned the work of local artists. These patrons shifted from the Viscontis and D'Estes of Italy to the aristocratic families of Paris and then to cities in Languedoc. The French card makers may have found an opportunity to imprint the tarot cards with their own set of messages and symbolism. There, the tarot would have found popularity beyond the aristocratic families into the world of the artisans and craft guilds. These groups had strict rules of initiation and guarded their secrets well. Some were known to have associations with local heretics. Weavers, for example, were notorious for their Cathar affiliation. It is not difficult to imagine secret messages of the tarot being preserved within groups such as this. And with the introduction of wood-block printing in the fifteenth century, tarot decks would have become more available to the less privileged classes.

In any event, it seems clear that the Tarot of Marseilles had its roots in the Italian Visconti-Sforza tarot. Although they differ in the quality of their artwork—the hand painted Italian cards being more elaborately detailed than the coarser woodblock style of the Marseilles decks—the two display similar images and common themes. As the tarot evolved from the Italian decks to the Tarot of Marseilles, it was able to drop certain symbols and images which no longer had significance to the new card makers. For example, many of the cards in the Visconti-Sforza deck show family crests and emblems, like the pattern of three interlocking rings, the Sforza fountain and Visconti shield, and the banner with the words *a bon droit*, "by good right," possibly referring to the Sforzas' right to rule Milan. In fact, since we don't see the substitution of similar images of the French aristocracy in the Tarot of Marseilles, we could conclude that the use of symbols and images meant to praise its patrons was not as important to the French card-makers as it was to their Italian counterparts. Although a hint of heresy may have already been placed into the Italian decks, it was only when the tarot developed into its Marseilles style that we see a more evident and complete expression of its underground theme.

Other changes differentiate the two styles of tarot. For one thing, the French added titles to the cards, which were absent from the earlier decks. In addition, there is no existing evidence of The Devil or The Tower in the Visconti-Sforza tarot. Either these cards were lost or they were never part of the deck in the first place. One theory is that they were omitted because of their negative or destructive themes. However, if that was so, we need to ask why The Hanged Man (sometimes known as The Traitor) was left in.

The three of coins, from the Visconti-Sforza tarot, with the words "A Bon Droit" on the banner. Courtesy of U.S. Games Systems, Inc.

As was common for artists of the Middle Ages, the creators of the Tarot of Marseilles were not necessarily looking to invent a completely new system of images. They were content to borrow and reinvent what was already in use. As one scholar points out, "There seems to have been little regard for originality [in medieval art].... In art, the achievements of the past were continually being consulted, absorbed, reinterpreted, and brought to new relevance in the works of the present."[83] In the same light, the creators of the Tarot of Marseilles were comfortable borrowing ideas, images, and themes from the Italian decks. However, as it became necessary to introduce new meaning and personalities into the tarot, new images, distinct from their former counterparts, were incorporated into the cards. For example, it is suggested that the two people on The Lovers in the Visconti-Sforza tarot may be Francesco Sforza and Bianca Maria Visconti, who bonded the two families together with their marriage in 1441. It would make sense that these two people lost their significance to the creators of the Tarot of Marseilles as other historical personalities were chosen from their own story. Thus, in The Lovers, card VI, the two figures from the Italian deck are replaced by three figures from the Albigensian story (which will be addressed when we get to the card in Part II).

Even the court cards of the four suits may have been meant to represent actual figures from the Albigensian campaign. It is possible that some of the nobility who supported Count Raymond VI, such as Raymond Roger of Foix, King Pedro of Aragon, Raymond Roger of Trencavel, and the Count of Commings may be represented in the four suits. Another possible historical reference is that the suits represent the four Cathar dioceses designated by Nicetas in 1167: Toulouse, Albi, Carcasonne, and Agen. (William of Puylaurens identifies the four Catholic dioceses in the area as Albi, Rodez, Cahors, and Agen.) In addition, the four queens, which were not part of the earliest examples of playing cards, may have been added to honor some of the women who played important roles in the Albigensian story. We will become acquainted with a few of these personalities when we visit The Empress. In the meantime, these references should remind us of the importance of the function of the tarot as a potential storehouse of historical information.

Over the centuries following the introduction of the Marseilles deck, the symbolism of the tarot has changed significantly. Many of the images were altered to satisfy the imaginations of new artists and to accommodate the visions of occult practitioners. It may be surprising to some readers of this book, therefore, to learn that the tarot originally had no association with fortune-telling or the occult. Kaplan tells us that the "impetus to occult interpretations of tarot cards was started by Court de Gebelin in France in the late eighteenth century; prior to this date *tarocchi* cards appear to have been used mainly as a game or as pictorial representations of noble families and their surroundings."[84] It would seem fair to say, then, that the Tarot of Marseilles had no major occult significance when it was first created.

When we speak of the tarot today, many people think of the Rider-Waite deck, produced by A.E. Waite and illustrated by Pamela Coleman Smith. This was the first deck to portray the number cards of the four suits in pictures and is probably the most popular deck available today. The artwork is impressive and includes both ancient religious symbolism and Christian imagery. However, the deck is a result of modern interpretation and was first published in 1910. Both Waite and Smith were members of the Hermetic Order of the Golden Dawn, a society of twentieth century occultists. Believing that he was rediscovering the true esoteric meaning of the cards, Waite said that the tarot "embodies symbolical presentations of universal ideas, behind which lie all the implicits of the human mind, and it is in this sense that they contain secret doctrine."[85] But Waite had Smith create a new tarot deck according to his own intuitive visions. In fact, the Golden Dawn encouraged each of its members to create their own deck of tarot cards to be used as tools for their own personal transformation. The end result was an interesting exercise in creativity, but it departs from the original historical messages of the Tarot of Marseilles.

The Nine of Wands, from the tarot deck of Pamela Cole Smith and A.E. White, first published in 1910.

More decks would follow in the spirit of modern occultism, including Aleister Crowley's Thoth deck, which introduced Egyptian symbolism based on his theory that the tarot evolved from Egyptian sources. Later, Carl Jung would associate the tarot with his concept of a universal archetypal unconsciousness. With Jung, the tarot images became a system for psychological interpretation, in a sense becoming a source of subconscious projection through common symbols. However, reading the tarot cards using this psychological approach poses a problem, as the symbolism becomes more of an exercise in free-association and loses its connections to actual history. In other words, it becomes too easy to say, "The Star means hope," or "The Tower means upheaval," and then move into a stream of personal intuitive or subconscious expression. This is not unlike reading a Rorschach ink-blot test. Everything becomes an acceptable interpretation. There are no incorrect answers. In a way, "reading" the tarot can become an interesting and often revealing journey for those seeking such processes. This is not to say that there is anything wrong with using the tarot for fortune-telling or other occult purposes, or even for personal exploration. Such activities have become a popular and fascinating practice. However, we should understand that these modern interpretations may have little to do with unveiling the tarot's true identity.

The tarot has definitely undergone numerous changes. Symbols of the four elements (earth, air, fire, and water), the signs of the zodiac, the four cardinal virtues (hope, charity, faith, and prudence), and numerous pagan deities have all found their ways into tarot decks. For the sake of brevity, however, we will skip a detailed investigation into the evolution of the tarot in order to focus on the story at hand. What is important to our current investigation is to discover why certain images in the Tarot of Marseilles have been altered or left out while others remain. This will give us important clues to the secrets hidden within the cards.

PART TWO

—

The Cards

Introduction

❦

*All the darkness in the world cannot extinguish
the light of a single candle.*

—St. Francis of Assisi

In this section, some of the information presented in Part I will be explored through the Tarot of Marseilles. The story comes to life through the personalities hidden in the cards. Count Raymond VI, his son Raymond VII, Bishop Fulk, Simon de Montfort, Pope Innocent III, and "Papa" Nicetas, the heretic preachers, the noblewomen of Languedoc, and the wandering Perfect all emerge from the tarot's disguise. Along with these historical references, the spiritual messages of the Cathars are also revealed in the images on the cards.

The tarot—acting like a set of flash-cards—reflects the events which inspired its creation. Every image on the cards was taken from a religious tradition of precise symbolism. At the second Council of Nicea, in 787, it was declared that "a picture is not to be fashioned after the fancy of the painter, but according to the inviolable traditions of the Holy Catholic Church."[86] As Mâle explains, "The art of the middle ages is first and foremost a sacred writing of which every artist must learn the characters."[87] In this way, medieval art became a form of medieval literature where the reader would be able to discern the artist's symbols just as he would read the words of a book. During the Renaissance, artists began to move away from this strict formula and devise other ways of representing their art. It is within this period of time that the creators of the tarot discovered a way of representing their clandestine messages within the cards. The tarot, therefore, must be viewed in light of both its traditional heritage and the new methods of artistic vision.

We must proceed with the assumption that every detail of the tarot has a symbolic significance. In the Middle Ages, numbers had special qualities, bordering on the supernatural. St. Augustine had stated, "Divine Wisdom is reflected in the numbers impressed on all things."[88] The creators of the Tarot of Marseilles surely would have been aware of this when they introduced the numbers to their cards. Therefore, we must not forget to take into account the potential significance of the numbers of the cards in our examination of the tarot. Even the major colors used in the cards may not have been selected by chance. For example, the three major colors used in the Tarot of Marseilles, gold, red, and blue, are the colors of the noble banners of Languedoc.

The heretical nature of the Tarot of Marseilles has already been mentioned. The presence of The Popess (a blatant affront to the Roman Catholic Pope) and the lack of images of Christ or the crucifixion raise questions of a heretical theme. It is clear that the tarot includes images that don't necessarily reflect the orthodox values of art in the Middle Ages. The presence of The Popess is evidence enough of the deviation from this standard. We might also add that The Wheel of Fortune, although a traditional symbol of the time, is recreated in the Tarot of Marseilles with animal figures instead of humans, thereby suggesting the heretical theme of transmigration (discussed again when we get to the card). In addition, it is clear from sermons as early as 1500 that the tarot was considered evil contraband by the Roman Catholic Church: *There is nothing so hateful to God as the game of Trumps {the tarot} ... for Trumps are said, so it is believed, to have been given their names by the Devil.... In it not only are God, the angels, the planets, and the cardinal virtues represented and named, but also the world's luminaries, I mean the Pope and the Emperor, are forced, a thing which is degrading and ridiculous to Christians, to enter into the game.*[89] The fact that the Church was so vehemently against the game of the tarot may not simply have been due to the inclusion of The Pope and other revered images but to its popular use—that is, in the manner in which people gathered to share its heretical ideas.

O'Neill has considered the connection between heretical sects and the tarot. "The heretical sects," he writes in his *Tarot Symbolism*, "were known to the tarot designers and incorporated into the symbolic system." Although he acknowledges the influence of heretical sects in the tarot, O'Neill denies the specific connection of the Cathars to the creation of the tarot and offers several arguments to that effect. To begin with, he doubts that the Cathars would have used such a system, since they believed that all material things, being of this world, are evil. Once we look at the reality of how the Cathars actually lived their lives, however, we get past these strict philosophical concerns. Although it is true that the Cathars considered material things to be the work of the devil (according to their belief in dualism), they still had to function in the real world. As practical people, they used material things just as everyone else did and were known to accept gifts of food, clothing and even money. In fact, most Cathars were involved in worldly pursuits. Biller tells us that many Cathars were from aristocratic families, well educated and held positions as notaries, doctors, lawyers and merchants.[90] Italian Cathars were known to have sent their initiates to the University of Paris, in order to learn scholastic logic. They possessed books and often carried copies of the New Testament and the Gospel of John with them, which they used in their ceremonies. Cathar texts also exist, such as *The Book of Two Principles*, written by an Italian Cathar in the thirteenth century. Another example of their literature is a ten volume book about Cathar beliefs written by John of Lugio, an ordained Cathar bishop. Therefore, it is doubtful that the Cathars would have denied another way of promoting their teachings, even if it appeared in the form of a deck of cards. In addition, it is important to consider that the Tarot of Marseilles was not necessarily created by the Cathars of the thirteenth century themselves, but rather by sympathizers who lived years later, during the fifteenth century, when that form of the tarot was produced.

O'Neill also argues that the Cathar involvement in the development of the tarot is inconclusive since the heretical theme of dualism is not present in all of the cards. Clearly, a dualistic theme can be seen by the presence of opposing forces in some of the cards such as The Sun and The Moon,

The Emperor and The Empress, and The Pope and The Popess. And there is also a heretical nature to The Devil (seen is his pagan attire), suggesting the creative force of all evil which the dualists held in opposition to the supreme God. But we must remember that the tarot was used as a source of other information, both spiritual and historical, and not just as a record of Cathar dualism. Preservation of the events of the Albigensian Crusade, for example, may have been as important to the creators of the tarot as maintaining the Cathars' philosophic teachings. As some cards reveal heretical messages, others were created to relate historical events or significant personalities. Therefore, the presence of dualistic or heretical images does not have to be evident in every card in order to prove the significance of Cathar involvement. In the end, O'Neill states that even though we may never entirely know what the creators of the tarot had in mind, "It's a great historical detective story."[91]

In addition, we can find evidence of a heretical theme in the Tarot of Marseilles not in what we see on the cards, but in what we don't see. Specifically, the lack of images of Jesus or the crucifixion suggests a shift from the orthodox teachings of the Roman Catholic Church in the fourteenth and fifteenth centuries, when an emphasis on the Passion of Christ became a focal point of Christianity. As we will see in our evaluation of The World, the image of Jesus is missing even in this card, where we would expect to find him at the center of the mandala. Other traditional symbols of Jesus such as the fish or the lamb are also absent in the tarot's set of images. One might infer that some images such as the lamp (light) held in The Hermit may represent Jesus, but these are minor references, if at all, and don't take the usual central place of honor shown in other religious art of the time.

It may be significant to note that the human figures in the first part of the major arcana are the dominant features of the cards, indicating the importance of the personalities in those cards. In contrast, the latter part of the major arcana moves into more religious themes, incorporating a variety of other images to portray its messages. These images work together to become the symbolic expression of the Cathar doctrine, especially in relation to the salvation of the soul.

We should also note that the placement of the first card of the major arcana has sometimes been altered. Some designers of tarot decks have put The Fool at the beginning of this series. It is sometimes placed there to represent the lowly, "foolish" individual at the start of his spiritual journey. In our story, however, we shall take the artist at his word and start with card number 1, The Magician. We will discover that The Fool takes his rightful place at the end of the deck—arriving there as the spiritual messenger and wandering priest.

Lastly, some of the images, even within the tradition of the Marseilles style of tarot, were changed from one card maker to another. The cards I refer to the majority of the time are from the Nicolas Conver deck. However, in a few specific cases, other Marseilles decks, such as those by Dodal or Noblet, are employed and noted when used.

The Magician (Le Bateleur), from the Tarot of Marseilles
by Nicolas Conver reproduced by France Cartes.

The Magician
I

౿

But there was a man named Simon who had previously practiced
magic in the city and amazed the nation of Samaria,
saying that he himself was somebody great, to whom they
all gave heed, from the least to the greatest, saying, this man
is the great power of God. And to him they had regard,
because for a long time he had bewitched them with sorceries.

—Acts 8:9-11

In the Christian tradition, Simon Magus, or Simon the Magician, was called the Father of Heresy. He was given this title after being accused of attempting to purchase the power of the Holy Spirit from the apostles for his own personal gain. From this we get the term "simony," the sin of buying spiritual favors or the selling of ecclesiastical offices. The lesson to be learned from Simon Magus is not just one of corruption and greed, but also about the folly of expecting personal salvation through any means other than righteous living, according to the teachings of the apostles. We are taught that spiritual power used for personal gain stems from vanity and pride, which are two of the mortal sins that prevent us from realizing our true spiritual nature.

Legend tells us that Simon was a master magician and showman. It is said that he was even able to fly—something quite believable in a world where magic and miracles were accepted as common occurrences. He claimed to be the messiah, and this may have been the root of his undoing. In the end, Simon was exposed as a false messiah, drunk on his own vanity. It seems he was nothing more than a simple street magician. As we will see, the task of the medieval magician— the Christian magus—was to transcend the limitations of the ego, thereby avoiding the perils of Simon's heresy. Interestingly enough, Simon Magus was also known as the Father of Gnosticism.

By the Middle Ages, simony had been declared a serious heresy. Lea describes the problem of simony as "the corroding cancer of the church throughout the whole of the Middle Ages ... from the pope to the humblest parish priest."[92] The Church, however, was reluctant to punish this crime. Despite its rampant abuse, not one person was ever charged with the crime of simony by the Inquisition in all of its years of activity.

To arrive at a full understanding of The Magician, we must look at several aspects of the card. The first involves an understanding of medieval magic, which was an important part of medieval science. Magic at that time was a function of man's place in the universe, and was therefore a part of astronomy, which was synonymous to astrology. In fact, the two approaches to the study of the stars, astronomy and astrology, didn't become separate sciences until the time of Galileo in the sixteenth century.

The fall of Simon Magus. Stained glass from Notre Dame de Chartres. Photo courtesy of Philip Maye.

During the fifteenth century, when the tarot was being developed, Europe was rediscovering the so called mystery religions of ancient Greece and Egypt. The hermetic traditions were being revived, and with them, the concept of the Christian magus—or magician—was developed. Hermetic writings were translated into books like the *Corpus Hermeticum,* which provided instruction on how to proceed along the magician's path. In effect, the role of the Christian magus was to negotiate the bridge between the outer cosmos and his earthly existence.

According to medieval hermetic theory, the universe consisted of three levels. In his book, *The Philosophy of Magic,* Arthur Versluis explains this complex cosmology: "There is the world of images—earth—above which is the realm of the planets, and then that of Essences.... Man was created in the image of the highest, the Divine sphere, passed through the celestial sphere of the planets and constellation, where he gained the proper aspect from each of the planets."[93] From there, he descended to earth into the realm of life and death. This lower, worldly nature is where the aspects of the ego exist. It was believed that upon death, some souls can ascend back through the planets and return to the highest realm, where they can relinquish their lower, transient nature and become reunited with God. As Francis Yates explains, "The dignity of Man as Magus, as operator, having within him the divine power, and the magical power of marrying earth to heaven rests on the Gnostic heresy that man was once, and can become again through his intellect ... a divine being."[94]

The magician was charged with the task of uniting the "essences" of the heavens with those of the earth by drawing the spirits down from the stars—a process known as sympathetic action. In order to accomplish this, he was required to have knowledge of astrology and the "natural correspondences," which represented the connections between man and the attributes of nature, angels and demons, gods and planets. The end result of this form of magic was the spiritual unification of the subjective life with the objective realm. In a sense, magic transformed the magician's internal experience through the manipulation of his external world.

In this first card of the major arcana, the Christian magus is shown in a mystical stance, raising his wand to call down the spirits of the astral bodies. For him, the celestial bodies of Jupiter, Mars, Venus, and the Sun are gods to be negotiated with. They each have their own correspondences with the material things of this world, and to help in his task, he employs the talismans on his table. They are his alchemical tools if you like. We see displayed before him the four elements: Earth (the circle, or coins), Air (the sword), Water (held in cups), and Fire (represented by the wand). Three of them lie on the table. He is holding the fourth (the wand) in his left hand. Traditionally, the wand, or baton, was a symbol of power normally held by the kings and lords of the land. But the Magician has snatched it up from the table and holds it up as if commanding authority from above. He who knows these magical secrets must surely control power. This is not unlike the symbolism of the bishop's staff, with its claim of divine right.

At some level, the Church must have appeared to have its own form of magic. People were confronted with the mystery of the high priest through his use of the sacraments, the function of the Eucharist, and the sanction of miracles. In the thirteenth century, magic and religion were intimately bound. Baptism, for example, was thought to prevent one from being drowned or eaten by wolves.[95] In a practical sense, then, it was the priest who served as the real magician.

The word "magician" comes from the Latin *magus*, which referred to the priest of the ancient Persian fire-cult of Ahura-Mazda.[96] And this leads us to the first major revelation of the Tarot of Marseilles—heretical as it may seem to most traditional tarot interpretation—that the Magician is the priest. However unorthodox this may seem at first, we can begin to see the identity of the Magician as the priest, revealed through the clever use of disguise, when we examine the card within the context of our story.

In medieval Europe, the most powerful representative of the Church at the local level was the bishop. Other than the pope, he was the Church official who was given the greatest legal authority and had the power to make life and death decisions. During the Albigensian Crusade, the bishop of Toulouse was Fulk of Marseilles. Fulk became bishop in 1206 and held that office until his death on Christmas day in 1231. Fulques, as he was often referred to earlier in his life, was born to affluent parents in the year 1150. He became a *jongleur,* a troubadour or street performer, while still a young man in his twenties. His reputation grew as he traveled through Languedoc, performing for the courts of Raymond V of Toulouse and Raimond-Roger of Foix.

Perhaps not coincidentally, another name used in the tarot for The Magician was *Le Jongleur,* or The Juggler. In the tarot, the Magician and the *jongleur* are treated like the great and powerful Wizard of Oz. Although he assumes a position of authority and awe, he is eventually discovered to be a peddler of illusion. In the Middle Ages, *jongleurs* were generally outcasts and looked down upon by the Church. Although official decrees were issued condemning them and forbidding them entry into the clergy, that policy was often overlooked. Such was the case with Archbishop Berengar of Narbonne (1190–1212), a man denounced by the pope for his notorious greed and corruption, who was known to allow monks to take on the work of *jongleurs* as extra jobs.[97]

No one knows why, but in 1195, at the age of forty-five, Fulques gave up his life as a troubadour and joined the Cistercian Order of monks. He carried the pope's banner in his fight against heresy and quickly rose to the appointment of bishop of Toulouse. Now known as Bishop Fulk, he became a staunch supporter of the French forces during the Albigensian Crusade and raised his own band of followers against heresy under the name of The White Brotherhood, or The Brotherhood of Toulouse. He was a close associate of Simon de Montfort and was present as an advisor at the battles of Lavaur and Muret. For his support, Montfort rewarded him with gifts of land. Bishop Fulk was also responsible for giving Dominic de Guzman a small hospice in Toulouse, thereby establishing the first Dominican house, later to become a major center of operations for the Inquisition.

Due to his strong position against the Cathars, Bishop Fulk was not well-liked by many of the citizens of Toulouse. On at least one occasion, they shouted that "he was not their bishop, but rather the 'bishop of devils.'"[98] In 1215, the Count of Foix, one of the strongest opponents of the crusaders, accompanied Raymond VI of Toulouse to Rome to discuss the abuses and misfortunes of the people of Toulouse at the hands of the clergy. In his address to the pope, he spoke of Bishop Fulk as "more like an anti-Christ than Christ's ambassador."[99] From these recorded statements, it is not hard to imagine how Fulk created a reputation of animosity in Toulouse's large population of Cathar sympathizers. And it may have been the intention of the creators of the Tarot of Marseilles to use the *Jongleur* to cleverly disguise Bishop Fulk in this first card.

If we consider all the elements of the images in The Magician, we can see another clue to the nature of this card. As mentioned earlier, every detail on the cards should have a significant meaning. Therefore, the small plant placed under the figure of the Magician should also impart symbolic value. Although it is difficult to identify the exact type of plant depicted, we notice it has thorns or nettles. Mâle explains that in medieval art, "Nettles denote the rank growth of evil."[100] A character was often identified by the association of an object of significance near or under the figure. In this case, the placement of a plant with nettles may help indicate the sinister nature of the Magician.

The troubadour, Folquet of Marseilles, Bishop of Toulouse. Reproduced by permission of the Bibliotheque nationale de France.

On a spiritual level, The Magician—seen here as the Christian magus—sets up the process of personal transformation in the tarot and prepares us for the journey through the rest of the cards. The Magician's number is I, the first card of the tarot, and The Fool (0) is seen in its proper place at the end. As the Magician moves toward the Fool, his spiritual transformation, represented by their numbers, is completed. One, representing the individual or the ego, eventually arrives at zero—the "nothingness" described in Buddhism where the individual experiences spiritual enlightenment, or ego annihilation, and at the same time attains an affinity with everything. The universal quality of the human condition allows for comparisons of the Cathar religious experience to Buddhism. For example, many reports exist which recall the deep meditative practices of the Cathar Perfects. Apart from the spiritual experience, it is the cultural differences which cause the two traditions to part ways.

In most traditional interpretations, the Magician represents the young man at the beginning of his spiritual journey. As everything is laid out upon the table in front of him, he can choose his own destiny. In his right hand he holds a coin or a ball—at the center of the card—representing his position at the center of his world. He is the individual, the ego apart from the rest of the world.

The shape of the coin is the circle ("0" or zero)—the sign of the Fool—and thus, we find another clue to the connection between the Magician and the Fool. We can also find other evidence of this link between the two. We see, for example, that the Magician's head is cocked to the right, the same as the Fool's, except that the Fool is looking upward in hope, instead of downward in doubt. The Magician's tools are revealed, while the Fool's are concealed in his pack. In the Conver deck, the Magician's shoes are yellow (which represents the intellect), whereas the Fool's are red (representing fire or transformation). We also see that the Magician is presented as a young man, while the Fool, sporting a beard, has become older and wiser.

The Magician and The Fool are placed at the opposite ends of the major arcana. The tarot shows us that man's spiritual progress from Magician to Fool is a journey from vanity to humility—the two qualities which, in the eyes of the Cathars, stand on opposite ends of the spectrum of human vice and virtue.

In the game of tarot, or *Tarocchi*, still played in parts of Europe today, the trumps appear in the order of their importance, from lowest to highest. That is, the higher numbered trumps have more trick-taking power. In this sense—although he appears to be in a position of importance—the placement of The Magician at the beginning of the trumps indicates a relative lack of power. This also suggests that the "higher" spiritual cards trump the lower numbered cards of the earthly stations.

The Magician is the poster-child for the spiritual journey through the tarot. It is the story of how Simon Magus, first presented as the *jongleur*, becomes Simon, the Father of Gnosticism.

The Popess (La Papesse), from the Tarot of Marseilles
by Nicolas Conver reproduced by France Cartes.

The Popess
II

⌒

He {Jesus} composed a more spiritual gospel for the use of those who were being perfected.... It was most carefully guarded, being read by those who are being initiated into the great mysteries.

—From a letter written by Clement of Alexandria in the third century

Historically, there is no evidence of a female pope. Therefore, it is curious that this card was included in the tarot. There was, however, a legend of a female pope named Joan that became quite popular from the thirteenth century on. Joan was said to have been the pope around 1099, during a time when there were several "anti-popes" who challenged the authority of Rome. Legend has it that Pope Joan became pregnant and delivered a child during a procession through the city, revealing her identity as a woman. Because this spectacle was unbecoming of the holy office, she was publicly stoned to death. Although the legend may not be supported by fact, it did have a significant cultural impact. In 1601, Pope Clement VIII may have inadvertently given the story a degree of credibility by officially declaring it to be untrue. To the masses, the legend of Pope Joan became an anti-papal satire and survived as a political slur against the official pope. After all, it was said, the Church seemed to have gotten along just fine during Joan's reign.

From the earliest appearance of the card, The Popess has indicated a heretical theme and implies a challenge to the pope's authority. Moakley tells us that The Popess may have been a reference to Manfreda Visconti, a first cousin of Matteo Visconti, who became a patron of the early Italian tarot decks. Manfreda served as the abbess of the *Umiliati* order of nuns, and was declared Pope of Milan in 1300. In the Visconti tarot, she is pictured in a nun's brown habit rather than a pope's gown. But because The Popess wears a three tiered tiara, we might assume that she is being portrayed with the same level of authority as the Roman Catholic Pope.

The Popess is represented by the number two. In the numerology of the Middle Ages, two referred to the dualistic nature of human beings, which proposes that we are composed of both spirit and matter. The idea is based on the notion that our spirit was created from the heavenly realm above and yet is bound to the temporal world through our material body. This establishes a dynamic struggle within us. This reference connects The Popess to the dualistic and heretical beliefs of the Cathars. More evidence of the heretical nature of The Popess can be found in the mere fact that she is a woman. Unlike the Catholic Church, which taught that women (starting with Eve) were the source of evil in this world, heretical groups such as the Cathars often elevated women to positions of importance, even allowing them to preach. Some became Perfects themselves and organized homes for other Cathar women. This was thought to reflect the attitudes of the original Christians. In the Gospel of Mary, for example, Jesus told Mary Magdalene that both men and women are ordained to speak when divinely inspired by the Holy Spirit.[101] In the Gnostic traditions, which taught the inner mysteries of Christianity, importance was placed on the Divine Feminine, or Mother Goddess. However, they explain that the supreme female figure was not the ultimate god, but rather one who had significant power here on earth. In this sense, The Popess may represent the Cathars in this earthly realm.

Curiously, the Popess is shown with an open book on her lap, unlike her depiction in the Visconti tarot where the book is closed. In the thirteenth century, William Durandus wrote of the symbolism of church art, suggesting that an apostolic figure depicted with a book indicates perfect knowledge, and that it is sometimes shown open "so that in it everyone may read."[102] Furthermore, in early Christian art the apostles were often shown holding an open book which identified themselves as teachers of the gospels. If this reference in The Popess reflects a similar imagery, then we might infer that the Popess is holding a book of spiritual teachings, even, possibly, of a heretical nature.

Of course, the book could also refer to a specific piece of writing, though we have no way of knowing its true identity. But if this is the case, it would probably be one of the common "heretical" books known at the time. If the book refers to the Book of Life—commonly associated with the final judgment of mankind—its meaning may be found in a message relating to man's ability to influence his own fate by leading a good life and refraining from sin. In effect, life is an "open book." Here, the Popess is saying that man possesses a degree of personal power to write his own story. This challenges the Church's explanation of God's secret plan, which will be revealed only at the final judgment. In this sense, the information in the book is being made available for all, and not just the select few in the hierarchy of the Church.

It is also possible that the book she is holding represents a heretical text such as The Secret Gospel of John, sometimes used in the Cathar ritual of the *consolamentum*. The veil on the card suggests that the book holds hidden teachings available only to those who are able to understand the Greater Mysteries. Of course, other messages could be associated with the card, as the teachings of different books may have been referenced.

The Empress (L'Imperatrice), from the Tarot of Marseilles
by Nicolas Conver reproduced by France Cartes.

The Empress
III

෬෯

*We are not entitled to deprive heretics of the life which God
has given them simply because we believe them to be in the clutches
of Satan.... Those who are our enemies on earth may, by
the grace of God, be our superiors in heaven.*

—Waso, bishop of Liege, 1045

In the tarot, The Empress represents the ultimate expression
of the medieval woman, both temporally and spiritually. The
images of women in the tarot are significant, as shown by
the inclusion of The Popess and The Empress as well as the
virtues of Temperance, Justice and Force. In fact, it would not
be surprising to discover that the addition of the Queen to the
four suits of the original deck of playing cards was a result of
the impact women had around the time of the Albigensian
Crusade. McGinn says that "it is only after 1200 that women
begin to take a prominent place in the mystical tradition....
Nothing is more striking about the new mysticism beginning
about 1200 than the important role that women assume."[103]

It would seem only natural for the creators of the Tarot of
Marseilles to recognize the women who played an important role
in supporting the Cathars during the Albigensian Crusade. In its
historical sense, then, The Empress may represent one or more

of the female matriarchs of Languedoc, such as Esclarmonde, the sister of the Count of Foix. She became an important Cathar Perfect and received the *consolamentum* in 1205. This illustrious ceremony was attended by most of the country's nobility.[104] Esclarmonde built schools and hostels to shelter Cathars and was known as their greatest patroness. As heiress to the Montsegur castle, she was responsible for its refortification and repairs. In the years after the Albigensian Crusade, the castle at Montsegur served as a safe-haven for the Cathar elite and became the site of their pivotal loss to the French crown.

Another famous matron of the day was Blanche of Laurac, who was called the "greatest matriarch of Languedoc Catharism."[105] Her town of Lavaur was the home of the Cathar bishop of Toulouse and has been described as "the very seat of Satan and capital of heresy" by those who conquered it.[106] Two of Blanche's daughters became Perfects, and one ran a Cathar home. In 1211, Blanche's only son, Aimeri de Montreal, was killed in the battle of Lavaur along with four hundred Cathars who were burned there. After the battle, an additional eighty knights were hanged, and Blanche's daughter, the Lady of Lavaur, was thrown down a well and covered with rocks.

It's very possible that The Empress was meant to represent one of these notable matriarchs. In addition to these individual historical references, however, The Empress (like many of the other tarot cards) also has a significant spiritual meaning. The Empress's number, three, is the number of the trinity and refers to all things spiritual. To grasp this meaning, it is important to understand the extent of the role that religion played in the medieval world. In simple terms, the life of the average person in the Middle Ages was permeated with religion and prayer. The crosses on the tops of churches could be seen from almost everywhere in every town. Relics of saints kept in some churches established a sense of importance for the local parish. Each craft guild had its own patron saint whose feasts marked the calendar of the year, and every child was given a guardian saint at birth. Their blessing brought the promise of security for the common man and woman. St. Barbara averted lightning, St. Medardus controlled the rain, St. Genevieve protected against fever, and St. Apollina cured the toothache. But the pinnacle of all sainthood was the Virgin Mary, mother of Jesus.

Saint Mary was the highest symbol of virtue, humility, and compassion. By the twelfth century, her veneration had grown into a widely popular cult. And although the Virgin Mary was an important figure in orthodox Christianity, the cult of the Virgin was a product of the masses, taking on an appeal of its own. To many Christians of the high Middle Ages, Mary represented the most personal aspect of the trinity. In effect, praying to the Virgin gave man his greatest chance of redemption and forgiveness of sin. John Shinners writes that, "Mary was like a kind-hearted noblewoman who could bend her son's ear in favor of her clients and shower them with his gifts.... By the twelfth century the Virgin Mary's growing cult as the queen of heaven enshrined her in the popular religious imagination as an intercessor so powerful and so appealing that she often threatened to supplant the Almighty. Religious art, architecture, literature, and especially private and public prayer all celebrated her nurturing role as the mother of God and patroness of humanity."[107] Her popularity is evidenced by literary works such as St. Bernard's

Homilies in Praise of the Virgin Mother, a book of poems dedicated to the Virgin Mary written in the twelfth century. Reverence of the Virgin Mary was seen everywhere. In his book, *The History of the Church in the Middle Ages*, Logan writes that "Every cathedral in France, no matter what title it had previously, became a cathedral dedicated to Notre-Dame"—Our Lady, as the Virgin was referred to in France.

In the Tarot of Marseilles, the Empress is shown facing forward on her throne, in the traditional position of power. Depictions of the Virgin Mary in this regal pose are common in medieval art and can be found in hundreds of examples in French churches and cathedrals. One of the most beautiful and inspiring of the twelfth century French cathedrals is Notre-Dame de Chartres, also dedicated to the Virgin Mary. In a large stained-glass image at Chartres, sometimes referred to as the *Belle Verrière,* the mother of Jesus is shown crowned and in her royal attire, with the baby Jesus on her lap. This depiction is similar to her crowned pose in The Empress, except that in the tarot card the baby Jesus is replaced by the emperor's shield. For the Tarot of Marseilles, this substitution may be seen as a shift in the significance of the image of the son of God to the values represented by the phoenix on the Empress' shield, a symbol of resurrection and hope. It may also suggest the position of the Virgin Mary as the true Empress of the world. The fact that the image of the Virgin Mary is being used in the tarot instead of images of Christ may in itself be evidence of heresy, as the Church resented all attempts to place the Mother on equal status as the Son.

(Interestingly, if we lay the cards side by side, we can see that the eyes of the Empress are diverted to her left, toward the Emperor. This may suggest the direction of sympathy or a blessing from the Queen of Heaven toward the Emperor).

"Le Belle Verrière," stained glass of the Virgin Mary in Majesty, from Notre Dame de Chartres. Photo courtesy of Philip Maye.

The association of The Empress with the Virgin Mary can also be found in the language of the literature of the times.

For example, the expression "Virgin Empress" appears in *The Song of the Cathar Wars*, written by witnesses of the Albigensian Crusade. In one verse, the author writes: "But by Saint Mary, Virgin Empress, I would rather die by the sword and shining steel than let them keep us crushed and helpless."[108] Here, the two names are written as if they are interchangeable—in effect, one and the same. It is likely, then, that the expression "Virgin Empress" was used as a popular term of endearment for the Virgin Mary. It should be noted that while most of the records of the time were written by church clerics, the author of this part of the *Song* is one of the only sources we have from the point of view of the Albigensians. Additional examples of this literary adoration of the Virgin Mary can be found in the poetry of the twelfth and thirteenth centuries, including the expression "queen of heaven" and *Imperatrix supernorum*, or "Empress of the highest."[109] For example, in the so called Marian antiphons, monastic hymns sung daily in monasteries, she is referred to as the "queen of heaven."[110] It seems reasonable, therefore, that the Virgin Mary found her place in the tarot under her alternate name, the Empress.

It should also be noted that the Cathars identified their sect with the Virgin Mary. Records of the Inquisition speak of this association: "They [the Cathars] deny that the Blessed Virgin Mary was the true mother of our Lord Jesus Christ.... But they say their sect and order *is the Virgin Mary* [my italics]."[111] The Cathars were also known to hold large feasts for the Virgin in which "Saint Mary and the God of the Cathars were both honored simultaneously."[112] This association may have been a factor in the tarot's inclusion of The Empress in the cards.

The Empress's number is three, described by Cavendish as the "reconciliation of opposites that produce a new unity."[113] *In the tarot, she is found sitting between the polar forces of The Popess and The Emperor—defining a new place of leadership. We can visualize this in her number, written as III, which is descriptive of three pillars. In the tradition of the mystical Hebrew Kabbalah, later associated with the tarot, the attribute of Beauty (tifereth) sits centrally between the left and right columns of the Tree of Life. If we allow ourselves the latitude to use this association then, we might say that The Empress also represents the principle of spiritual Beauty as she sits on her throne.*

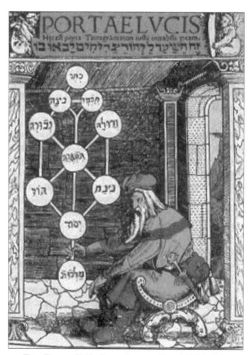

The Tree of Life from the medieval Kabbalah.

Examining the card from a different perspective, we can see that the Empress holds a shield emblazoned with a phoenix with raised wings—the symbol of one who will rise again. Her shield, along with the orb-topped scepter, is comparable with the symbols shown on The Emperor, which ties them together in theme as well as in name. These symbols, which represent temporal power, connect the Empress to this world. However, since there was no actual empress in the history of the Albigensian Crusade, we need to look at an alternative use of such an image. The empress is a common image in medieval art. Sekules informs us that "personifications of *places*, whether cities or countries, *especially as regal or armed women*, are one of the oldest forms of power symbolism [my italics]."[114] Seen in this sense, The Empress becomes the allegorical representation of the most important city in the Albigensian saga—the city of Toulouse. As we can see, the tarot cards offer a variety of different meanings. The images may have been used to describe different information, depending on how the story was being told.

Although there is good cause to believe that The Empress may have been associated with the Virgin Mary and the patronesses of Languedoc, we cannot dismiss the possibility of the card's reference to Blanche of Castile, who married King Louis VIII and became Queen of France in 1223. Since her son, Louis IX (later St. Louis), was only a child of ten at that time, Blanche served as his regent and remained in charge until her death in 1252. As regent, she was effectively the most powerful person in France. (The imperial shield on the card clearly indicates the distinction of one who had the power to rule.)

Blanche was on the scene and played an important role during the last years of the Albigensian conflict. She was also instrumental in preventing the marriage of Raymond VII to a younger woman who could have borne him a son to inherit his estate (see the discussion under The Lovers). Queen Blanche was surely one of the most influential figures of thirteenth-century France, and therefore, we can not exclude her in our historical review of The Empress.

This does not discount the association of the card to the Virgin Mary, but simply suggests an additional or alternative reference of the card. It has already been suggested that several of the tarot cards had multiple references or different levels of interpretation, especially when a spiritual message is considered. What seems most evident is that the tarot cards were not meant to be taken at face value but were used symbolically to represent a number of personalities and themes.

The Emperor (L'Empereur), from the Tarot of Marseilles
by Nicolas Conver reproduced by France Cartes.

The Emperor
IIII

༄

Render therefore unto Caesar the things which are
Caesar's and unto God the things which are God's.

—Jesus, Luke 20:25

"Remember that the pillars which uphold the world are two: the one the Pope, the other the Emperor."[115] These words were spoken at the Council of Lyons by the German Patriarch, Berthold of Aquilar, in 1245. Such was the state of affairs in the political life of medieval Europe. The spiritual world belonged to the pope, who claimed his authority from Saint Peter, and the temporal world belonged to the Holy Roman Emperor, who inherited his power from Caesar. However, the line of separation between these two worlds was often blurred as the ambitions of the papacy routinely involved material and territorial issues. In 1300, Pope Boniface VIII changed the papal crown to the triple tiara, indicating his status as "high priest, king (of the Papal States), and emperor over the emperor."[116] Boniface's lofty ambitions were clear, as he pronounced that "It is altogether necessary to salvation for every human creature to be subject to the roman Pontiff."[117]

Perhaps the greatest of the Holy Roman Emperors was Frederick II (1194–1250). The son of Henry VI, Emperor of Germany and Sicily, Frederick lived during the Albigensian Crusade. As a young boy, he was left as the ward of the newly elected pope, Innocent III. By the time Frederick was chosen as emperor, it was evident that there would be tension between the two leaders of the Christian world. Innocent III made his position clear when he stated, "I am he who will judge all and be judged by none."[118] He once wrote to Frederick, warning him, "Do not usurp our office in things spiritual; be content with the temporal power which you hold from us."[119] On the other side of the conflict, Frederick's disdain for the papacy can be seen in a letter that he wrote to King Henry III of England:

> *Take warning from the past. Has not the unjust interdict of the Pope reduced the Count of Toulouse and many other princes to servitude? ... The whole world pays tribute to the avarice of Rome. Her legates travel through all lands, with full powers of ban and interdict and excommunication, not to sow the seed of the Word of God, but to extort money.*[120]

Even though the emperor still held a strong position in the Germanic states, other areas of Europe were ruled by local kings and princes. In Languedoc, the land was ruled by powerful families and noble lords, and during the Albigensian Crusade, the most powerful leader was Count Raymond VI of Toulouse. His family's influence extended to all parts of Europe through strategic marriages to the royal houses of England, France, and

Aragon (Spain). His vassals included some of the most powerful counts in Languedoc, including the Trencavels of Carcassone. Raymond also held lands under Frederick II.

The number of The Emperor is four, the number of the material world. On the tarot card, The Emperor, we see the dominant appearance of the eagle, the personal emblem of the Holy Roman Emperor, which was used historically as the symbol of worldly rule. In 1395, Giangaleazzo Visconti purchased the title of Duke of Milan from the Emperor Wenceslas of Germany and adopted the black imperial eagle as his coat of arms. The symbol of the eagle appears on the shields of The Emperor and The Empress in the Visconti-Sforza decks and was adopted into the Tarot of Marseilles. Other insignia of the office of Holy Roman Emperor (given by the pope to indicate the right to rule) included the sword, the scepter, and the golden orb surmounted by a cross—all of which appear on The Emperor card.

In his *Dictionary of Symbols*, Cirlot writes that in Christianity, "the eagle plays the role of a messenger from heaven.... In general, it has also been identified ... with prayer rising to the Lord, and grace descending upon mortal man."[121] In the Tarot of Marseilles, the Emperor's shield may be a statement of political loyalty in direct opposition to the pope and the king of France. This emblem of the Holy Roman Emperor may be a sign of Raymond VI's authority to rule Toulouse (taken away by the Albigensian Crusade), just as it gave the Visconti the right to rule Milan. In a spiritual sense, the eagle is symbolic of a messenger to God.

Most of the images of emperors in medieval art show them in full frontal view, which is a sign of power. Morris Bishop explains that one of the influences of Byzantine art on the West was their style of representing sacred figures: The "subjects, whether saints or emperors and their officials, are presented full-face, confronting the spectator."[122] Jesus, for example, was always shown facing forward in a position of power and authority. The Emperor in the Tarot of Marseilles, however, is shown in profile. In this case, the Emperor's position may be a reflection of his having been removed from his seat of power by the pope.

In the Tarot of Marseilles, as the two cards are laid out side by side in proper sequence, the Emperor has his back to the Pope, possibly in a pose of defiance. The depiction of the Emperor in profile may also represent the fact that Raymond VI was willing to show an acquiescent face to the Church while in fact opposing its authority, thus concealing his sympathy for the Cathars.

The Pope (Le Pape), from the Tarot of Marseilles
by Nicolas Conver reproduced by France Cartes.

The Pope

V

❧

We are no mere man, we have the place of God upon earth.

—Pope Innocent IV

In the fifth card of the major arcana, we see the Pope dictating orders to two figures kneeling in the foreground. As was the custom, the pope's legates, or ambassadors, traveled in pairs. As we explore the characters within the context of our story, we will see that these two men represent a number of possible characters. For example, shortly after his election in 1198, Pope Innocent III sent his two Cistercian legates, Rainer and Brother Guy, to Languedoc to fight heresy there. The two figures may also represent Bishop Diego of Osma and Dominic de Guzman (who later became St. Dominic), also sent by the pope to preach against heresy in the area. Or perhaps they are Peter Seila and William Arnale, the first two inquisitors sent to Toulouse.

Another possibility is that the two monks on the card are Peter of Castelnau and his fellow Cistercian, Ralph, sent to Toulouse in 1203 by Innocent III to urge Raymond VI to expel heretics from his territories. The murder of Peter of Castelnau was used to incite the French forces into a crusade against the Albigensians. These two figures may also represent the two patriarchs of Constantinople and Jerusalem who were called by

Innocent to attend the Fourth Lateran Council in 1215. There they defined heresy, reestablished the power of the Church, and proclaimed the new rulers of Languedoc. In a broader sense, the two figures in this card might even refer to the Franciscan and Dominican monks who knelt before the pope to obtain confirmation of their orders. Unfortunately, we are once again stymied by the lack of recorded evidence and must allow ourselves to indulge in a bit of speculation as to who might actually be represented.

In any event, the actual identities of the two figures do not change the underlying meaning of the card. In fact, the characters referred to by the two figures in front of the Pope may have been changed at times to include different versions of the story being told.

O'Neill argues that certain cards such as The Pope are inconsistent with the Cathar point of view and therefore refute the theory of the tarot being created by Cathar sympathizers. He seems to feel that since The Pope represents the opposing force of the Church, it should not have been included in a Cathar-based system. However, the tarot should not necessarily be taken literally, at face value. In O'Neill's own words, "In the tarot and in the age when they were designed, one can expect that many orthodox symbols will be deliberately inserted into the system, just to deceive the casual observer."[123] In the case of The Pope, it would not be surprising to find that a case of parody or disrespect is being implied in the card, since the inclusion of the pope's image in a set of playing cards was seen by the Church as offensive. It was for this reason that The Pope was removed from some of the later decks such as the Minchiate Tarot in the 1700s. We can not disregard the fact that it may have been intentionally placed in the Tarot of Marseilles for the same reason. Even the number of the card may imply a slur on the papacy. In the tarot, The Pope is the fifth card of the major arcana, corresponding to our five fingers, five senses, and five extremities (legs, arms, and head)—in other words, the attributes of the average man, not of God. "Traditionally," explains Cirlot, "the number five symbolizes man after the fall."[124] Looking at it from this point of view, it seems that the Pope has been displaced in the tarot from his otherwise lofty position.

We must also keep in mind that the tarot may have used traditional images of medieval art to present or even disguise heretical messages. Given the heretical nature of the tarot, The Pope may also have another, more clandestine, meaning. In medieval culture, the Latin word *papa* was used to indicate an ordinary priest. Runciman reminds us that there were a number of heretical 'popes' in Bulgaria. "It was probable," he explains, "that it [*papa*] was used as a title for priests coming from one of the Eastern heretical churches."[125] In this case, The Pope might represent Bishop Nicetas of Constantinople, who came to Languedoc to share the Cathar message. The kneeling priests then would be the Cathar *filius major* and *filius minor*, his two appointed assistants. Another heretical image in the card is the presence of the twin pillars—a reference to Jachim and Boaz, the two pillars of King Solomon's Temple. They represent the dualistic nature of the world, the opposing forces of light and dark, which are a central theme for the Cathar faith.

An interesting play on numbers can be seen with cards IIII and V. The challenge of power between pope and king came to a head in the early fourteenth century when Boniface VIII, one of the most arrogant and corrupt popes of the Middle Ages, declared the clergy exempt from royal taxation. King Philip IV of France responded by sending a small force (headed by the grandson of a man who had been burned as a heretic in Languedoc) to abduct the pope. Boniface was imprisoned, where he remained until his death shortly thereafter. Philip then installed his own pope, Clement V, in Avignon rather than in Rome. This shift in papal power, which began in 1305, lasted until 1417 when the Council of Constance installed the new pope in Rome.

This period of papal exile in France opened up an era of corruption that might have shocked Simon Magus himself. Clement's reputation landed him a role in Dante's Inferno as one of the popes accused of simony. The new "anti-pope" was by all accounts a puppet of the French king. Twelve of King Philip's associates were appointed as cardinals, and other clerical positions were sold to the highest bidder. In addition, all tithes collected by the French clergy were to be paid to the crown.

Could King Philip IV and Pope Clement V have been intentionally included in the tarot? It may not be coincidental that the card numbers of The Emperor and The Pope, four and five, match those of Philip and Clement respectively. This clever play on numbers would be consistent with a sense of political satire, albeit in hidden form.

THE TEMPLAR CONNECTION:

Another infamous claim to fame of King Philip IV and Pope Clement V was their participation in the demise of The Knights of the Temple of Solomon, more commonly known as the Templars. The Templars were a paramilitary order sanctioned by the pope in 1129, supposedly to provide safety for those traveling to Jerusalem during the Crusades. Another version of the story is that they were sent to Jerusalem to retrieve a treasure buried underneath King Solomon's temple. In any event, by the thirteenth century, the Templars had become one of the most powerful organizations in Europe. At one point, they owned approximately nine thousand properties and estates throughout Europe. They were the personal bankers of Henry III of England and held the crown jewels in their Paris depository as collateral. In France, they served as the royal treasury and held the notes to substantial debts owed by the king. The Templars even served as bankers to the pope as early as 1163.

At the beginning of the fourteenth century, Philip IV of France found that he was broke and in debt. Philip "The Fair" (as he was called after his handsome appearance) is said to have thought of himself as "the 'most Christian' of Christian Kings."[126] On Friday, October 13, 1307, he ordered the mass arrests of the Templars on trumped up charges of heresy. Pope Clement V was pressured to go along with his plan. In 1312, he disbanded the Templars and many were sentenced to death. Their Grand Master, Jacques de Molay, was executed after being tortured and held in prison for six years.

Interestingly, Count Raymond VI had a close relationship with both the Templars and the Hospitallers, another order of Christian knights. Although both the Templars and the Hospitallers played an important role in the earlier crusades to the Holy Land, neither one fought with the crusaders against Count Raymond in the Albigensian campaign. In fact, Templar knights were said to have ridden with the king of Aragon in defense of Toulouse against Simon de Montfort when the city was attacked. Both the Templars and the Hospitallers had set up houses in Toulouse. By 1200, it is likely that there were many close family ties between the Templars and the Cathars of Languedoc.

When Raymond VI died in 1222, he left a large amount of money to the Templars and Hospitallers of Toulouse. Since Raymond was denied a Christian burial, his body remained in the hands of the Hospitallers, who retained his skull as a relic.

The Lovers (La Moureux), from the Tarot of Marseilles
by Nicolas Conver reproduced by France Cartes.

The Lovers
VI

❦

He that hath a wife and children hath given hostages to fortune.

—Francis Bacon

Although The Lovers was carried over from the earlier Italian tarot, the images on the Tarot of Marseilles card were significantly altered to give it a new meaning. And remaining consistent with our assumption that the images in the tarot were done intentionally, we should not simply regard this as an arbitrary change. Just as the two figures in the Visconti-Sforza tarot are said to represent the marriage of the two Italian families, the figures in the Marseilles deck similarly point to historical figures within the Albigensian story. In addition to this change in personalities, we notice that a third figure was added to the card in the Tarot of Marseilles.

Raymond VII—the son of Count Raymond VI of Toulouse—didn't have any male heirs. This meant that there would be no one to carry on the family name or inheritance. To make matters worse, as part of the treaty which ended the Albigensian Crusade, his only daughter, Jeanne, was promised in marriage to Alphonse, one of the sons of the French king. Both children were only nine years old at the time. Since

Raymond's current wife was past childbearing age, his only hope of securing his legacy as ruler of Toulouse was to obtain a divorce and remarry a younger woman who could bear him a son. But his attempts to find a new bride were foiled twice by fate—first, when the pope died before he could grant an annulment of his marriage, and again when Count Raymond Berengar of Provence unexpectedly died before he was able to fulfill his promise to give Raymond the hand of his daughter, Beatrice. Raymond appealed to Blanche of Castille, the French regent, to intervene with the new pope on his behalf. Blanche had her own agenda, however, and arranged for Beatrice to marry her youngest son, Charles. The significance of this action was profound, as Raymond was effectively denied a male heir. In 1271, his daughter Jeanne and her husband Alphonse died childless, thereby leaving Toulouse to France. (We will revisit Alphonse and Jeanne when we look at The Sun, card XVIIII).

In this card, The Lovers, we see Blanche of Castille as the older lady on the left, intervening between Raymond VII, the man in the middle, and Beatrice, the young lady on the right. Thus, The Lovers adopted a piece of history which became forever encrypted in the Tarot of Marseilles.

In another sense, The Lovers is a card of choice. In fact, as the card was altered in the Marseilles decks, it was often referred to as the Two Paths.[127] Here, the man in the middle must choose between the matriarchal figure on his right, representing the institutional Church, and the fair maiden on his left (the side of the heart), representing Love. Fortunately, he is assisted by the angel above, who points his arrow at the young maiden.

The Chariot (Le Chariot), from the Tarot of Marseilles
by Nicolas Conver reproduced by France Cartes.

The Chariot
VII

∽

For whoever exalts himself will be humbled, and
whoever humbles himself will be exalted.

—Matthew 23:12

The Chariot in the tarot has usually been associated with triumph. In earlier decks, the figure riding in the chariot was shown as a woman. However, in the Tarot of Marseilles, the image has been changed to a man. In the art of the Middle Ages, a masculine figure usually represents a specific person. In the context of our story, the triumphant warrior shown on this card is Simon de Montfort, the hero of the northern crusaders. His conquests became legendary, as he imposed fear and terror to everyone in his path. Eyewitness stories of his battles were chronicled by the monk, Peter of les Vaux-de-Cernay. In his *History of the Albigensian Crusade*, Peter included many examples of miracles to enhance Montfort's reputation and show his favor in God's eyes. Upon his return to Paris during a respite from battle, Montfort was said to have been greeted as a hero and celebrated with a grand triumph.

Montfort was awarded the title of Viscount of all of Languedoc and Lord of Toulouse by the pope at the Fourth

Lateran Council in 1215. Due to his inability to gain full control of Toulouse, however, he was unable to attain final victory. In the end, Montfort's glory was cut short when he was killed while besieging the city of Toulouse. (Additional details of his death will be noted when we discuss card XI, Force.)

> *In the Conver Chariot the shield bears the initials V.T. This space is normally reserved for the initials of the artist or woodcutter. For example, the Chariot's shield in the Noblet deck is inscribed with the initials I.N., which stand for Jean Noblet (I and the J being written the same). In his deck, Nicholas Conver's name appears on the two of coins, while the person represented by V.T. in Conver's deck remains unknown. Is it possible that the initials on this card may stand for Simon Montfort, Vicompte de Toulouse, or Viscount of Toulouse?*

In addition to the historical references mentioned above, The Chariot contains spiritual messages as well. The number seven has been thought to be a very spiritual number. Seven, "composed of four, the number of the body, and of three, the number of the soul—is preeminently the number of humanity, and expresses the union of man's double nature."[128] In this sense, we see the ultimate challenge of the soul where the two forces collide. The number seven relates to the spiritual realm, referring to the seven gifts of the Holy Spirit and the seven days it took God to create the world. On the other hand, seven also pertains to the realm of man on earth, as there are seven virtues and seven deadly sins.

This moral battleground is represented in The Chariot in the form of Simon de Montfort. Appearing as the triumphant charioteer, he represents pride and vanity—considered the worst of the seven deadly sins. The rise and fall of Simon de Montfort is symbolic of one who seeks personal power with disregard to others. In the end, we learn that it is man's pride and vanity which attach him to his own sense of self-importance, thereby distancing himself from God. As we shall see in card X, Fortune has an effect on all things temporal, as the triumphant Charioteer is brought down from his lofty perch.

Curiously, the character in this card does not appear to be in control of his chariot. He is holding no reins, and the horses seem to be drawn in opposite directions. In the animal world, the horse represents work. He does the work of man, just as man does the work of God. The wheels in the background are also facing in opposite directions. (This has been altered from the images in earlier decks, which show a normal looking chariot). This odd visual image conveys the message of the false sense of triumph which comes from human vanity. The message is that God holds the reins, and only by conforming to the will of God can man truly triumph.

The spiritual message is clear. Although we have the ability to choose good or evil, our Chariot will be stuck going nowhere—as this tarot card shows—if we decide to live in opposition to the spiritual laws of the universe.

Justice (La Justice), from the Tarot of Marseilles
by Nicolas Conver reproduced by France Cartes.

Justice
VIII

❧

We must conquer the world, sin, death and the devil, not with
material swords and spears, but with the sword of the
Spirit, which is the Word of God.

—John Bunyan,
The Pilgrim's Progress

Depictions of the virtues were common in medieval art. They acted as allegorical lessons in the fight against the opposite force of the vices. The architecture of twelfth century cathedrals such as the Notre Dame de Paris, for example, is adorned with the enduring figures of both virtues and vices. At the head of the battle for good, we find Humility (*Humilitas*) in the war against Pride (*Superbia*). In effect, the virtues personified man's struggle for the salvation of his soul. According to Aristotle, Justice, Force, and Temperance (represented in the Tarot of Marseilles) are three of the four cardinal virtues. Wisdom, the fourth virtue, may likely have been depicted as The Hermit. Although the images of the virtues were commonly found in various orthodox sources, they are adopted by the tarot as messengers of moral instruction. As we mentioned earlier, the Tarot of Marseilles was not looking to create a new set of images, but rather sought to use the existing ones to suit their purpose. The inquisitor, Bernard Gui, explains: "among the first things which the [heretics] ordinarily tell and teach their believers are some precepts which seem good and moral, such as to practice virtues and good works, [and] to avoid and flee from vices."[129] As we will see, the "virtue" cards relate information about the history and sentiment of the time in addition to their moral function.

In other tarot decks, the three cardinal virtues, Temperance, Justice, and Fortitude (Force), are commonly found in different positions within the order of the major arcana. This tells us that their location in the deck was not as important as the moral values they represent. In the Tarot of Marseilles, the order of the virtues is presented as Temperance, Justice, and Force. Coincidentally, this is also the three-stage process which the Church took in its campaign to subdue heresy. At first, the pope and his representatives resisted forceful action and attempted to convert the heretics by sending monks into the area on preaching missions (Temperance). Then edicts were declared, making heresy a spiritual crime deserving of ecclesiastical punishment (Justice). And lastly, since the first two approaches failed, a more violent approach was used in the form of the crusades (Force). Thus, the position of the three virtues in the Tarot of Marseilles is arranged in an order which helps relate the story being told.

In addition to the cardinal virtues of Temperance, Justice, and Force, the three theological virtues of Humility, Faith, and Charity are often found in medieval art. It is possible that these theological virtues are represented by the first three cards of the major arcana: The Magician (with his downward glance), The Popess, and The Empress, respectively. Although women are commonly used to represent the virtues, The Magician, here representing humility, is a man. However, Sekules explains that "in the visual arts, independent traditions allowed their gender to be varied depending on their purpose and context."[130] (In the same way, The Hermit may represent Wisdom.)

In the medieval world, justice was not necessarily kind or compassionate. The image of the upright sword on the card indicates a swift and lethal—if not militant—punishment for those who break the law. Christians learned from the Old Testament that even God's justice can be cruel and violent. In medieval art, the sword was commonly associated with martyrdom. This could be a reference, then, to the many Cathars who willingly chose a horrific death rather than renounce their faith. These Cathars may have risen to this status not unlike the Christian martyrs who, through death, became saints in the Catholic Church.

For medieval man, there were two forms of justice—spiritual and temporal—just as there were two different types of crimes. The former signified the higher justice of heaven and the latter referred to the lower justice of earth. Spiritual justice referred to the final justice of God, where all men are ultimately judged, while temporal justice is derived from the word *Justitia*, which refers to a worldly sense of moral behavior. In establishing a sense of social order, temporal justice implied the right for some to impose punishment for crimes committed under the law of the land. This right was normally reserved for the lord or ruler, who had the power of life and death. "Medieval political structure was ideally a contract exchanging service and loyalty in return for protection, justice and order."[131] The breaking of this social contract was grounds for declaring injustice. (This understanding of medieval justice will be significant when we look at the actions of Raymond VII in The Hanged Man). Justice, as *Justitia*, also describes a holy way of life without the need for sacraments. It points to a movement away from formalized religion and presents morality as personal responsibility.

In this card, the chair appears to have been drawn with angelic wings, suggesting that Justice is of a heavenly nature and has a spiritual meaning. It becomes the task of man to grasp her lessons here on earth. But when man acts as his own judge, he is limited by his very nature, for his justice is impeded by his ability to comprehend spiritual truths and distinguish good from evil—something which has become obscured as it is filtered through the human brain. As it is written in the Wisdom of Solomon (9:13), "For what man is he that can know the counsel of God? Or who think what the will of the Lord is?"

By eating from the Tree of Knowledge (of good and evil), man broke his covenant with God. In a moment of vanity and righteousness, he claimed to know right from wrong, and for this, he was banished from the Garden of Eden. He exchanged his condition of "at-one-ment" with God for a lifetime of seeking "atonement." In acquiring knowledge, man became like the gods. But it is also this very knowledge which separated him from God. In a sense, then, knowledge became the root of all evil, and therefore the realm of the devil. The horrible events witnessed by the Cathars during the thirteenth century must have served to reinforce their dualistic belief in the evil nature of this world.

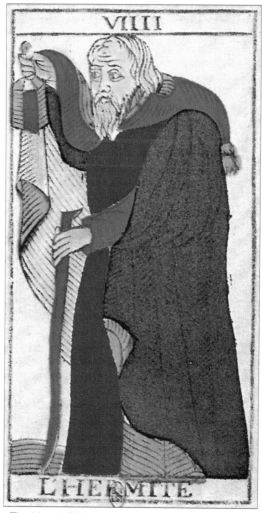

The Hermit (L'Hermite), from the Tarot of Marseilles
by Nicolas Conver reproduced by France Cartes.

The Hermit
VIIII

༄

Jesus said, if thou be perfect, go sell what thou hast and give to the poor, and you shall have treasure in heaven, and come follow me.

—Matthew, 19:21

There is a story from the twelfth century that tells how Valdensius of Lyons was so impressed by the words of a *jongleur* that he gave all of his real property to his wife and donated the rest of his possessions to charity. He retained a degree of practicality by keeping enough money to purchase translations of the Bible in the local vernacular, which he used to educate the poor. Rejecting the wealth and pomp of the Church, he spent the rest of his life preaching to his countrymen. Because of his life of strict poverty, his followers were sometimes called the Poor of Lyons, or simply the Waldensians. As one author put it, "The development of his ideas marked the flowering of a 'free market' of spiritual choice and a lethal threat to the established Church."[132]

Along with Valdensius, the twelfth century was witness to many other dissenting evangelists. Wandering from town to town, these holy men lived the lives of ascetic hermits, challenging orthodox religious ideas which often labeled them as heretics. Peter of Bruys was one such man. A critic of the Church, he was often found preaching in the countryside around Toulouse and along the trade routes between Italy and France. Peter was an ordained Catholic priest, but lost his position in the Church when he began burning crosses, declaring them as empty icons. Arnold of Brescia was another wandering priest who preached the virtues of poverty as he attempted to live an apostolic life. We also hear of the wealthy Pierre Mauran of Toulouse, who was so admired by the Cathars there that he was nicknamed John the Evangelist.

But of all the heretical preachers who wandered through Languedoc in the Middle Ages, the most influential was probably Henry of Le Mans. Henry the Monk, as he was referred to, traveled to Toulouse after being thrown out of Le Mans for preaching against Church policies. Like Peter of Bruys, he drove people away from the Church by pointing out its corruption and erroneous practices. Many of his ideas were compatible with those of the Cathars. He preached the emptiness of the sacraments and infant baptism and rejected the notion of original sin. In all cases, he looked to the gospels for support. His most challenging ideas, however, involved the notion that the role of the priest and the institutional Church were not necessary for personal salvation. Henry believed that only prayer was essential. He considered his authority to preach to be divinely inspired, stating, "I obey God rather than man."[133] His preaching was based on the message of love and he stressed the importance of personal strength and perseverance in attaining God's blessings.

Henry's following was so impressive that Bernard of Clairvaux, the greatest preacher of his time, traveled to

Languedoc in an attempt to suppress his growing movement there. In 1145, Bernard wrote an angry letter to Count Alphonse Jordan of Toulouse (Raymond VI's grandfather) regarding the situation:

> We have heard of the great evils which the heretic Henry inflicts every day in this Church. He is now busy in your territory, a ravaging wolf in the guise of a sheep.... We can tell what sort of man he is by his fruits: churches without people, people without priests, priests without the reverence due to them, and Christians without Christ.... the sacraments are not considered sacred ... the grace of baptism denied.... When he was chased from France for his wickedness, the only territory open to him was yours. Only under your protection could he ferociously ravage Christ's flock. [134]

These words may have been influential in convincing the Church to focus its attention on Toulouse, years later, during the Albigensian Crusade. Some records indicate that Henry was finally taken in chains to the bishop's prison, whereas others say that he was grabbed by a mob and burned in front of the church of Saint Gilles. Although the ideas of Henry the Monk, Peter of Bruys and others do not precisely mirror Cathar theology, their contribution to the broader dissent within the laity is undeniable and set the stage for others to follow.

Henry the Monk was described as a bearded man with long hair who often traveled barefoot. (Although we can't see the Hermit's feet in the card, he appears as a robed, bearded man with long hair.) Traditionally, Cathar Perfects wore black robes to indicate their status, and those who received the *consolamentum* were often called "robed heretics." Because of their similarities, The Hermit could have been used as a reference to the Cathar priests.

The Hermit is another card which has changed from earlier decks. In the Tarot of Marseilles, he is not "the Old Man" (*il Vecchio*) or Father Time of the Visconti-Sforza tarot. The hourglass of Father Time has become the lamp of the Tarot of Marseilles. While Dummett feels that this change was due to a misunderstanding by the new artists, I believe that the earlier images were quite clear and that these changes were created for a specific purpose. Clearly, the card has taken on a more spiritual theme, as I believe the artists intended. The Hermit in the Tarot of Marseilles holds a lamp in his right hand, as if to say, "Let me show you the way." The fact that he is holding a lamp in daylight indicates that this must be a spiritual light.

The lamp, by the way, is another symbol for Jesus, who said, "I am the light of the world" (John 8:12). Although some might see this as a reference to Jesus, it would be a minor one in comparison to the larger scope of the spiritual messages of the Tarot of Marseilles, which are clearly of a heretical nature.

The Hermit, from the Visconti-Sforza tarot. Courtesy of U.S. Games Systems, Inc.

An interesting feature of this card is the style of its number. In the Tarot of Marseilles, nine is written as VIIII, instead of IX. This odd way of writing the number may have something to do with the combination of the two other cards, written similarly, which add up to nine—The Pope (V) and The Emperor (IIII). The message of The Hermit may point to the significance of combining these two cards of opposing power.

The Wheel of Fortune (La Roue De Fortune), from the Tarot of Marseilles
by Nicolas Conver reproduced by France Cartes.

The Wheel of
Fortune
X

૭૭

The time will come when every change shall cease,
this quick revolving wheel shall rest in peace.

— Francesco Petrarch, *I Trionfi* (fourteenth century)

According to the Cathar belief system, man undergoes a series of transmigrations on earth before reaching the Last Judgment. This concept of transmigration is somewhat similar to the Buddhist concept of karma, which teaches that good moral choices allow us to reach a higher state of transformation in future lives, while poor moral choices lead to a transformation into lower animal forms. Karma teaches us that whoever is attached to the earthly affairs of life rises and falls with the revolutions of the wheel of fate and fortune. The Cathars adopted this concept of the transmigration of souls from earlier sources. In the sixth century, Boethius wrote in his *Consolation of Philosophy*, "He who abandons goodness and ceases to be a man cannot rise to the status of a god, and so is transformed into an animal."[135] This may be why the figures on The Wheel of Fortune in the Tarot of Marseilles are represented by animals instead of the human figures we find in the earlier Visconti-Sforza decks.

The Wheel of Fortune, from the Visconti-Sforza tarot.
Courtesy of U.S. Games Systems, Inc.

Cathar philosophy expands upon this belief by stating that man can only survive beyond these limitations through the knowledge of his infinite spirit. In the Tarot of Marseilles decks, the figure at the top of the wheel wears a crown. However, his position is temporary. As all things inevitably change, even the king must fall. The lesson lies in the fact that the spiritual man is required to choose goodness, and in this way, he prevents himself from being drawn downward into the realm of base animal instincts.

In the Tarot of Marseilles by Conver, the Wheel appears with six spokes in the form of the *chi-rho*, the Christian symbol for Christ, adopted from an early pagan emblem consisting of the first two Greek letters of the word *Christos*. Although other tarot decks appear to show the usual eight spokes of a normal wheel, we can see upon closer examination that the horizontal spokes are in fact a part of the turning mechanism. This leaves us with the six spokes of the *chi-rho* once this horizontal bar is removed. The symbol of the *chi-rho* in the tarot places Jesus at the center of the Wheel of Fortune and indicates his detachment from the transformations of rebirth which revolve around him. Only one who has been enlightened can sit at the center, undisturbed by the incessant revolutions of the wheel.

The association to Jesus here does not contradict our earlier statements of his status or lack of importance in the tarot. In this instance, Jesus is being used for moral instruction, and is not being deified in the traditional orthodox manner. It was, after all, the moral teachings of Jesus that appealed to the Cathars, and not the Church's claims to his nature. The Wheel of Fortune is also a pivotal card of the tarot, as it begins a shift from the themes of the mundane world of the previous cards to the more spiritual realm of the ones that follow.

In medieval art, sacred numerology was often blended into the creative arts. It's possible to see some evidence of this in the tarot. Consistent with its image, The Wheel of Fortune has been placed in a pivotal position. Because of this, some cards can be seen to become curiously "transmigrated" through the deck, so to speak, by combining their numbers to that of The Wheel's. For example, if we combine the number of the Pope (V) to The Wheel (X) we arrive at XV, the number of The Devil. Considering the Cathars' view of the pope, this may not be just a coincidence.

We might find similar connections if we were to examine some of the other cards in this manner. For example, if we use this numerological tool to extrapolate the evolution of the Magician (I) around the Wheel, we see that he passes into the position of Force (XI) in its first revolution: X + I = XI. In that phase of evolution, he sits in power at the top of the world. But with another turn of the Wheel, he finds that in order to obtain real power, he must learn the higher spiritual secrets of The World (XXI): X + X + I = XXI.

Through the same process, The Empress (III) becomes devastated in Death (XIII), the two people from The Lovers (VI) are found falling from The Tower (XVI), the lamp of The Hermit (VIIII) has become transposed into the light of The Sun (XVIIII), and the lady in Force (XI) has become transposed into the spiritual realm of The World (XXI), with the lion now at her feet.

Force (La Force), from the Tarot of Marseilles
by Nicolas Conver reproduced by France Cartes.

Force
XI

∾

This liberty my father had always impressed on me, assuring
me that, with it and the will resolved to maintain it, I might look
on calmly, though the very vault of heaven gave way and
broke over my head, for I had nothing to fear.[136]

—Count Roger-Bernard II of Foix,
upon being forced to accept the terms of the 1229 Treaty of Paris

To discover the meaning behind the images on this card, we must look at them allegorically, as they were meant to be seen. In its most direct symbolism, the card represents the virtue of Fortitude, definitely something demanded of the southern forces in a time of war.

In its historical context, the lion in this tarot card symbolizes the enemies of the Albigensians. It may refer to King Louis VIII of France, who was called The Lion. It was Louis who launched the crusade against the Albigensians and brought defeat to Count Raymond VII. Although the symbol of the lion also referred to other figures of power and authority at the time—most famously Richard I, "Lionheart," of England—its association with Simon de Montfort may be the most relevant for the Tarot of Marseilles. The red lion was Montfort's heraldic sign and appeared on both his shield and his banner. William de Puylaurens wrote in his Chronicles that Montfort "rushed on the enemy like a lion."[137] Montfort is said to have been killed during a siege of Toulouse by a stone thrown from the tower by a mangonel, a wooden war engine used to hurl boulders. At the time, the walls of the tower were being "manned" by the women of the town. Therefore, although this card may appear to represent one of the cardinal virtues, it may also refer to the death of Simon Montfort, as shown by the force of the woman over the image of the lion.

The death of Simon de Montfort. Courtesy of Francis Guizot.

It appears that the Force card in the Tarot of Marseilles was altered to make a point. Whereas the earlier Visconti tarot shows Force as a man aggressively wielding a club, the creators of the Tarot of Marseilles changed the image to a weaponless woman in a less threatening pose. This implies a different, less violent type of force. It may signal the power of the weaker forces of the Albigensians dominating the French crusaders. Although this might have been wishful thinking on their behalf, given the outcome of the Crusade, it may nevertheless offer a symbolic picture of hope or strength. The card also calls to mind the image of an unarmed knight in combat with a lion, commonly thought of as "symbolizing chivalric courage."[138]

In a broader sense, then, we can say that the figures shown on card XI are symbolic of the two forces in opposition: the Cathars of the Church of Love (another name for the Cathar sect) and the ferocious crusaders (symbolized by the lion).

Force, from the Visconti-Sforza tarot. Courtesy of U.S. Games Systems, Inc.

Another clue to the association of Force to the Cathars lies in the sandal that the woman in the card is wearing, visible below her dress. Sandals were usually worn only by monks and others who accepted the ascetic lifestyle, making this figure a likely reference to the Cathar priest.

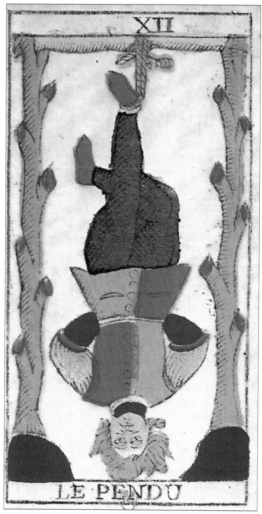

The Hanged Man (Le Pendu), from the Tarot of Marseilles by Nicolas Conver reproduced by France Cartes.

The Hanged Man
XII

❦

So at the bottom of the universe where Satan sits, in the lowest ring of all, traitors are laid to waste eternally.

—Dante, *The Inferno*

The Hanged Man in the tarot has sometimes been called The Traitor—an image most likely taken from the "shame paintings" of the time, in which a traitor was pictured hanging upside down by one foot. In a world where political and family bonds were vital to one's welfare and security, one's allegiance, given by the swearing of an oath of loyalty, was often a matter of life or death. To be a traitor to one's loyalties was a capital offense.

In the Tarot of Marseilles, this card may refer to a particular historical character or characters in the Albigensian saga. Depending on how the story was told, it could relate to a number of people. The Traitor could be someone like Arnaud Sicre, who first befriended but then turned against Guillaume Belibaste—one of Languedoc's last Perfects. Or it may refer to Raymond Gros, a trusted and beloved Perfect for over twenty years, who gave up scores of names to the inquisitors after going over to the Dominicans in 1237. Referring to Gros, Lea writes, "It is difficult to exaggerate the severity of the blow thus received by heresy by the conversion of this important person."[139] Still another infamous character in the Albigensian campaign is Count Raymond VI's own brother, Baldwin, who switched loyalties to fight on the side of the crusaders. When Baldwin was captured, Raymond had him hanged as a traitor, describing him as "far worse than Cain."

In our investigation of the characters represented by The Traitor, we cannot overlook Raymond VII. After becoming Count of Toulouse following the death of his father in 1222, Raymond attempted to carry on the fight against France and the Church. But he lacked the strength and leadership his father had shown, and in the end, he lost all of his father's territories and wealth to his adversaries. Of particular importance to the message of the present card, young Raymond didn't seem to have the same tolerance for the Cathar population that his father had shown. Caught between protecting both his Christian and heretic subjects (the two poles of *le Pendu*), Raymond was forced to make a choice—he had to give up one to save the other. His choice "lay between sacrificing one side or both sides, and what well might seem the lesser evil coincided with his own selfish instincts of self-preservation."[140] In an attempt to maintain what was left of his legacy, he chose to give in to the demands of Rome ahead of his loyalty to his own subjects. We might even say that his hands were metaphorically tied or that he was "hung out to dry," not unlike the figure on the card.

Ultimately, Raymond VII was unable to withstand the combined forces of France and Rome. Even his soul was threatened with eternal damnation as he found himself excommunicated by the pope. Seeing no other source of redemption, and concerned for the safety of his city, Raymond "begged for reconciliation to the Church."[141] His excommunication was finally lifted, and in 1229, he signed the Treaty of Paris, ending the Albigensian Crusade. As part of the Church's terms of the treaty, Raymond was forced to vow to persecute all heretics in his land and conduct an inquisition in the city. He showed his acquiescence to these terms in 1248 by ordering the burning of eighty convicted heretics. In addition, all of his officers were required to be "good Catholics," which meant that he could not hire Jews or Cathar sympathizers. He was also forced to make exorbitant payments to the Church, which left him all but bankrupt. In addition, he promised to go on a crusade to Palestine, but this was precluded by his death in 1249. Lea writes that the house of Toulouse "was thus reduced from the position of the most powerful feudatory, with possessions greater than those of the crown to a condition in which it was to be no longer dreaded".[142] Raymond's promise to step up the persecution of heresy in Toulouse must have had a significant effect on the population. To the *credentes*, those who were sympathetic to the Cathars, the young count must have truly looked like a traitor.

The number of the Hanged Man is twelve, which possesses a definite quality in the Middle Ages. Twelve is the product of three and four, which, if we recall from our discussion of The Chariot (VII), combines the spiritual with the material aspects of man. As there are twelve signs of the zodiac which bring order to the year, so did Jesus select twelve apostles to spread his word. Mâle tells us that "twelve is the number of the Universal church… of which the apostles are the symbol."[143]

Death from the Tarot of Marseilles
by Nicolas Conver reproduced by France Cartes.

Death
XIII

⚭

A scene of war indeed, when the killing was done—blood,
brain-matter, eyes and limbs, feet, legs and arms lay strewn
about, filling the roads and open ground.

—From The Song of the Cathar Wars[144]

Warfare in the Middle Ages was brutal by any standard. Terror by mutilation was probably more common in medieval battles than one might imagine. Armies responsible for such atrocities were sanctioned by the Church, blessed by the priests, and protected by the saints. Raymond of Agiles, in his description of the taking of Jerusalem by the Christians during the First Crusade, stated, "Some of our men cut off the heads of their enemies.... Piles of heads, hands and feet were to be seen in the streets of the city.... In the temple and porch of Solomon, men rode in blood up to their knees and bridle reins. Indeed it was a just and splendid judgment of God, that his place should be filled with the blood of the unbelievers."[145]

The battles of the Albigensian Crusade were no less horrific. Peter de Vaux-Cernay wrote, "Our crusaders burnt innumerable heretics with great rejoicing."[146] But the horrors of this war were not committed by only one side of the conflict. The fanaticism of the crusaders sometimes led to brutal retribution by the besieged. In one incident, the Count of Toulouse retaliated for earlier abuses by cutting off the hands and feet of his prisoners. More evidence of this gruesome treatment of prisoners was witnessed in the town of Minerve, where the locals "put out their eyes ... cut off their ears and noses and upper lips and sent them off."[147] The crusaders would retaliate a year later at Bram, where a hundred prisoners were allowed to leave town only after their eyes had been gouged out and their noses and upper lips hacked off. They were able to arrive at a town twenty-five miles away only because one man had been left with one eye in order to lead the others there.

Strangely, Death's face seems particularly macabre in the Tarot of Marseilles. Whereas earlier decks showed Death as a somewhat normal looking skeleton, the figure has changed significantly in the Tarot of Marseilles. Here, Death is pictured in profile, with one visible eye. The skeleton seems to have also taken on additional facial features on top of its bare skull, as if its lips were removed and its nose cut off (pictured in the card in a blackened outline). We shouldn't dismiss this as a result of the artist's poor drawing skills. It could just as easily be an intentional reference to the horrific events mentioned above.

The devastation took its toll on everyone in Toulouse. The fields and crops in the outlying areas were purposely destroyed—in effect, "scythed" by the northern forces. Charlotte Elizabeth, in her book about Count Raymond VI, could just as easily have been describing the thirteenth card of the Tarot of Marseilles when she wrote about the Albigensian Crusade: "No one can say what multitudes were brought to God in the course of that fearful struggle, what a harvest of souls was reaped for heaven in those fields of blood."[148] It is easy to see the similarities between the images of the battles of the Albigensian war and the body parts and scythed fields we see in the Death card of the Tarot of Marseilles.

Another curious feature of the face of Death in the Tarot of Marseilles is the crescent moon that outlines the back of his head. In medieval symbolism, the left-facing crescent represents one who has been honored by a sovereign. However, the "de-crescent," or crescent which has been turned 180 degrees (such as that seen in the Tarot of Marseilles card), implies evil, as the horns are turned in the sinister direction. This feature was not a part of Death in the earlier tarot decks and could have been added to illustrate the evil nature of the card beyond a simple representation of natural death or change.

In the Tarot of Marseilles, Death is the only card without a name on it. It's hard to believe that this would have been done without intention. One could imagine that a name was not placed on the card because Death is such a horrible concept. However, I believe that the creators of the tarot had another view in mind. As we are told, "In the beginning was the Word, and the Word was with God, and the Word was God." (John 1:1) The spoken word, then, is the creative force of the world. Giving something a name, in effect, is like creating it in reality. Giving Death a name, then, would be tantamount to admitting it exists. To the Cathars, however, death was not real. Only the body dies. This belief was important in supporting the idea that the spirits of the fallen Cathars survived. Even The Devil has a name on his card. To the Cathars, the Devil was very real. In fact, according to the dualist tradition, he created the world and everything in it. But Death was only part of this world. In this sense, this card contains its own spiritual quality.

Because of its historical significance, some might see a connection of this card to the Black Death, which wiped out almost half of the population of Europe in the fourteenth-century. Although this might sound like a reasonable interpretation, the image we see in this card doesn't resemble the depiction of the Black Death as it was usually shown in medieval art—a skeleton draped in a black cloak. It also doesn't explain some of the other images we see in this card, such as the scattered body parts. One thing that may be said regarding the Black Death is that it may have caused a renewal of the spiritual over the material, as many people saw it as retribution from God or a sign of His disappointment in His children. In this way, it may have fostered the growth of religious fever and increased piety in the surviving population.

Temperance (Temperance), from the Tarot of Marseilles
by Nicolas Conver reproduced by France Cartes.

Temperance
XIIII

൭

Are you able to drink from the cup that I drink, or to be baptized
with the baptism with which I am baptized?

—Mark 10:38

In Temperance we see another one of the cardinal virtues
included in the tarot. Although Temperance is traditionally
represented as a woman pouring what appears to be water
from one jar to another, she is shown here for the first time in
the form of an angel. In the Tarot of Marseilles, Temperance
is placed conspicuously between Death and The Devil. After
the horrific abuses of the Albigensian Crusade, as shown on
the previous card, a spiritual message is introduced to restore a
sense of meaning to life—a respite, if you will, from the harsh
realities of the world. Although the beneficence of Temperance
is followed by what looks to be another sinister card, we will
see that The Devil has a definite spiritual implication beyond
its evil appearance.

The vases are also important symbolically, and contain their
own spiritual value. In medieval art, "the empty vase symbolizes
the body separated from the soul."[149] In a spiritual sense, then,
the jars Temperance is holding signify the vessels of man's

physical body, the water, his spirit. The fact that the water isn't flowing vertically downward as it would if poured in reality gives us the notion that we are dealing with a metaphysical process. Catharism teaches that man's material body is filled with a divine spirit, and here we see the angel filling the vessels with this spiritual essence. This is a reminder that even though the physical body can be destroyed, the eternal spirit remains unscathed. In another sense, the pouring of the spirit from one vessel to another may also be a reflection of the transfer of the Cathar doctrine from one person to another, which was essential to its survival.

The Devil (Le Diable), from the Tarot of Marseilles
by Nicolas Conver reproduced by France Cartes.

The Devil
XV

༄

It is the spirit that gives life, while the flesh is of no avail.

—John 6:63

To medieval man, life and death were separated by a thin veil. The average person in the Middle Ages was preoccupied with the supernatural and the divine, and medieval art was an expression of the divine revelation. In such a world, the devil, demons, and angels were a very real part of his everyday world. As the Cathar Perfect, Guillaume Belibaste, wrote, "All the air is full of good and evil spirits."[150] Images of the devil in medieval art suggest his presence in the cultural psyche, and stories of his malicious deeds were accepted on faith. It was commonly thought, for example, that demons could fly overhead at night and steal the souls of the departed—a practice which could be averted by keeping a lock of hair from the deceased family member. The belief in the power of holy relics and magical talismans were methods man used to negotiate favor with the spirits of the other world. In medieval times, for example, "the girls of Languedoc used to put a drop of their blood or a nail-paring into a cake or a potion in order to make a boy fall in love with them."[151] Within this realm of designed reality the devil took center stage.

With this card, the Tarot of Marseilles makes its strongest statement of Cathar dualism. It speaks of the dual nature of man—his spirit trapped within his material body, shown on the tarot card by the man and woman in shackles bound to the devil. The antlers which the man and woman in the card are wearing add to this theme as they are reminiscent of the adornments used in the pagan festivals of the times to exemplify man's animalistic nature.

Any reference to a specific historical personality in this card would surely have to live up to the reputation of this ambassador of evil. Jacques Fornier, one of the most feared and infamous Inquisitors of his time, definitely fits the bill. Known to be an incorruptible official, he kept some of the most detailed records of inquisitional trials we have. As bishop of Pamiers, Fornier was responsible for hundreds of arrests, trials, and punishments of accused heretics. In 1334, he was elected pope at Avignon and took the name Benedict XII. His own records reveal that he was called "a devil of an Inquisitor" by his accused.[152] Of course, this statement may have simply been a coincidental choice of words, but it could also have reflected the thoughts and feelings of the general population. The use of this diabolical reference to Bishop Fornier in the tarot may have been quite appropriate in relating the abuses that took place under his watch.

But perhaps this label was too much for just one man to claim. It is just as likely that The Devil is associated with several contemptible personalities of the time. From the records of the Inquisition, we are told that the Perfect, Belibaste, made this statement: "There are four great devils ruling over the world:

the Pope, the major devil whom I call Satan; the lord King of France is the second devil; the Bishop of Pamiers the third, and the lord Inquisitor of Carcassonne, the fourth."[153] Statements such as this give us clues to the language and symbolism used at the time, and it would therefore seem reasonable that these expressions might be incorporated into the images used in the tarot. In fact, Ladurie reminds us that in the 1320s, the four powers named above came together against the Count of Foix, one of the last of the local nobility who offered resistance in support of the remaining Cathars.[154] It's possible that The Devil in the Tarot of Marseille represented one or more of these sinister characters in Belibaste's statement.

Some authors on the tarot have suggested that the two people standing at the front of this card correspond to the two lovers of card VI. This transposition of The Lovers into The Devil may be based on the Cathars' aversion to marriage, which was looked upon as another example of the base desires of the flesh which promoted the regeneration of souls into this world, and should therefore be avoided. The Cathar Perfects refrained from any physical contact with the opposite sex and taught that the desires of the body must be subjugated for the sake of the spirit. It was thought that in this way man can identify with his higher nature and prepare himself for the Final Judgment. Although this strict practice of abstinence was only observed by the Cathar Perfects, their message may have found its way into the tarot through the symbolic images of this card.

The Tower (La Maison Dieu), from the Tarot of Marseilles
by Nicolas Conver reproduced by France Cartes.

The Tower
XVI

ᕼ

*Towers will fall, and walls be razed to the ground, and you
will all of you be reduced to servitude. Thus, force will
prevail where gentle persuasion has failed.*

—Dominic de Guzman[155]

The Tower has an interesting historical significance. For one
reason, it does not appear in many of the earlier tarot decks.
Therefore, in order for it to be included in the Tarot of
Marseilles, it must have represented something of importance.
Clues to its significance may be found by looking at its style of
construction. The crown at the top of the Tower seems to suggest
that the Tower is round, although most of the earlier decks
show it as a square or rectangular building. The construction
of round towers was not common in Europe until the return
of the Templars from the Middle East in 1127. These temples
and churches, which can be found throughout France, served as
fortifications. The Tower of the Tarot of Marseilles, then, may
have been meant to represent a military structure.

The most prominent military outpost of the Cathar
resistance was Montsegur, in the county of Foix. In one
sense, then, The Tower symbolizes the castle at Montsegur.

The two men shown falling from the Tower are likely Ramonde of Pereille, who rebuilt the castle in 1204, and Peter Roger of Mirepoix, who was assigned as the castle's co-lord. Montsegur was a sanctuary for many of the Cathar perfects and bishops who had been forced to flee from their towns during the Albigensian Crusade. In 1232, Guilabert de Castres, the Cathar bishop of Toulouse, moved to Montsegur and established his headquarters there. After a few residents of Montsegur killed several of the pope's legates in a surprise attack, it became clear that the castle had to be taken by force if the heretics were to be subdued. The fall of Montsegur in 1244 is commonly accepted as the Cathars' final military defeat. Guilabert's successor, Bertrand de Marti, was burned alive after surrendering at Montsegur, along with over two hundred others who would not renounce their faith.

In addition to the card's reference to Montsegur, it may also be indicating a structure in the city of Toulouse. At the time, the largest tower in Toulouse was the bell tower at the Basilica of St. Sernin. This twelfth century cathedral was built to honor St. Seturnin, or Sernin (the first bishop of Toulouse who lived in the fourth century), who was martyred for his refusal to pay homage to the pagan gods. For this act of insubordination, he was tied to the back of an ox and dragged through the streets until his death. For many, the martyrdom of St. Sernin was a symbol of the willingness to accept death rather than reject one's faith—not unlike the Cathar heretics who inhabited the city centuries later.

The martyrdom of St. Sernin, reproduced by permission
of the Bibliotheque nationale de France.

If we look at a picture of the bell tower at St. Sernin, we can
actually see a similarity to the structure in The Tower of the tarot.
The tower at St. Sernin has five tiers, the lower three built in the
twelfth century and the upper two completed in the fourteenth
century. The spire at the top was not added until a century later. The
cathedral of St. Sernin was the most important religious building
in the city, and served as a rest stop for those making the sacred
pilgrimage to Santiago de Compostela in the northwest of Spain,
where the relics of St. James are said to be kept. The cathedral
of St. Sernin was also the site of the largest inquisition of the

Middle Ages, where almost six thousand inhabitants of Toulouse were interrogated between May 1245 and August 1246.[156] As an additional piece of our story, it is said that the stone that killed Simon de Montfort was thrown from the bell tower of St. Sernin. Therefore, we cannot dismiss the possibility that the tower of St. Sernin is represented as The Tower of the Tarot of Marseilles.

The bell tower at St. Sernin, photo by Cerideven.

Although The Tower is associated with the specific structures above, it may also have a general reference to the many towers seen in the city of Toulouse. As we discovered in Part I, Toulouse was the home of Count Raymond VI and became the strongest city of opposition to the northern forces during the Albigensian Crusade. The architects of Toulouse had built towers over its many churches and bridges. Private homes were also fortified with towers. In fact, more than three hundred private towers existed in 1226, even amidst the destruction caused by the war.[157]

Kaplan explains that towers "in medieval and Renaissance times were symbols of the power of aristocratic families."[158] According to the chronicler, William of Puylaurens, "when Simon de Montfort took over the government of Toulouse in 1216, he dismantled the walls, filled the fosses, and leveled the 'towers of the fortified houses in the town.'"[159] Thus, the Tower may be referring to the destruction of the towers, walls and noble houses of Toulouse. In this way, it became a symbol of the general spirit of resistance of the city. Consistent with this reference, then, the two figures falling from the tower would most likely be Count Raymond VI of Toulouse and his son, Raymond VII—represented by the toppling crown—who were toppled from the position of power they once enjoyed.

> *In earlier decks, The Tower was sometimes The House of God (le Maison Dieu). Before it took on that name, however, it was called The Devil's House and Fire. This evolution of titles seems to indicate a significant change in the meaning of the card from one of despair and destruction to one of spirituality or a higher power. The significance of one falling from the House of God might suggest a general spiritual decline, as seen in the days after Montsegur and Toulouse had been lost.*

The flames shooting out of the tower differ from one tarot deck to another. In some, such as the Tarot of Marseilles by Dodal and Noblet, they are rising from the tower. In other decks, such as the Conver tarot, a cloud-like fire seems to be coming down from above. The significance of these alterations may be associated with the artist's understanding of the source of destruction. Some decks show an arrow that looks somewhat like a lightning bolt pointing upward, away from the Tower, suggesting a reversal of natural forces. (Another earlier name for this card was The Arrow or Thunderbolt.)

Interestingly, there are no existing examples of The Tower or The Devil in the Visconti-Sforza Tarot. Kaplan surmises that the two cards would have had powerful negative associations for these families as The Tower implies destruction and The Devil is associated with bondage. If this is the case, then we must ask ourselves why these cards were included in the Tarot of Marseilles. After all, it's doubtful that their negative associations would have changed over the years. Perhaps it was because they were useful in telling the story of the pain and destruction which occurred during the time. After all, the illustration of The Tower does appear to evoke images of Montsegur, St. Sernin, and the towers of Toulouse.

The Star (Le Toule), from the Tarot of Marseilles
by Nicolas Conver reproduced by France Cartes.

The Star
XVII

෬

Like water spilled on the ground, which can not be recovered, so we must die. But God does not take away life; instead, he devises ways so that a banished person may not remain estranged from him.

—II Samuel 14:14

The Star sits at a point in the tarot in which the message of the cards shifts into a more spiritual phase. As we move away from the worldly images of historical figures (The Popess, The Empress, The Emperor, The Pope, etc), our focus is now turned toward the divine through the astrological bodies of The Star, The Moon, and The Sun.

In the Christian tradition, the star often represents the guiding light that led the magi to Jesus. It is a beacon of truth. We have already mentioned that to medieval man, the number seven was a spiritual number. But it also had significance in their cosmology, referring to the seven celestial bodies known at that time and what was known as the "eighth sphere," or the "heaven of the fixed stars."[160] Thus, in this card, we see the seven stars—the seven heavens—with the larger eighth sphere in the middle. It was believed that when one dies and is perfected, he passes back through the seven heavens and is reunited with God.

In earlier examples of this card, as seen in the Visconti-Sforza tarot, we are shown a solitary robed woman holding up a large star, thereby creating the central focus of the card on the Star as an astrological body. In the Tarot of Marseilles, however, the card is changed to show a naked woman kneeling by a river while pouring water (or spirit) out of two vases. With the inclusion of these other symbols, the meaning of the card is changed. In a similar fashion, the next two cards of the Tarot of Marseilles (The Moon and The Sun) have new images such as dogs, towers, crayfish, and children, which indicate a similar shift in emphasis from a purely astrological design to one which demands a broader scope of interpretation. In our discussion of The Moon and The Sun, we will discover the meanings of these new images and how they help tell the Cathar story.

The Star, from the Visconti-Sforza tarot. Courtesy of U.S. Games Systems, Inc.

As far as The Star is concerned, we need to look at the additional images on the card to help reveal its message. The change in her appearance, for example, may offer us some clues. For example, the woman shown on this card appears to be pregnant. However, pregnancy here is not likely a literal reference to the act of giving birth, since the Cathars denounced marriage, the bearing of children, and sexual activity. Rather, it suggests that the hopes and future of Catharism would have to wait, as in the gestation period of birth.

> *The symbolism of the pregnant woman on The Star may also be associated with the monastic tradition of helping those in need. One account from a German monastery says that "pregnant women were permitted to fish in the monks' brook; but they were allowed to do so only on the condition that they put one foot in the water and keep the other on land."[161]—similar to what we see in the card.*

The naked appearance of the woman (often associated with Venus) also aligns her with the ideals of purity and truth. She is seen pouring the contents of two vessels (which look similar to the ones we saw in Temperance) into a stream. This action symbolizes a return to the source. It is a card of hope. In the context of the Cathar story, the woman is pouring the Cathars' future hopes into the underground consciousness of the earth where it can be nourished and revived at some later time. The Star appears after The Tower—after the fall of Montsegur (and/or Toulouse). The Cathar elite have been killed and the counts of Toulouse defeated, but there is the hope that their souls and their teachings will survive. Borrowing from the symbolism of the time, The Star may also point to Raymond VI. When he returned to Toulouse to defend his city against the French army of crusaders, he was said to have been greeted as "the morning star, risen and shining upon us."[162] In this context, it is possible that the bird perched on a tree in the distance is actually the eagle which appears boldly on Raymond's shield.

However, the identity of the bird is hard to identify with any certainty. If it is actually a dove, then it takes on a completely different meaning. As we are told in Cirlot's *Dictionary of Symbols*, the dove represents spirituality. "Christianity ... depicts the third person of the trinity—the Holy Ghost—in the shape of a dove."[163] In this case, the presence of the bird in the card can be seen as the Holy Ghost, representing the words of the gospels, which the Cathars used as their main source of inspiration. As the Cathars believed that the words of the gospels were to be planted in the minds of others, we find that the trees in The Star will grow where the seeds are planted, watered, and nurtured.

If we carry this religious interpretation even further, we might ask if the landscape of the card could possibly point to the biblical Eden. Here, we would expect to see the two trees found in Genesis—the Tree of Knowledge, and the Tree of Life. As adopted from the early Gnostic teachers, the Cathars believed that those who attained knowledge (gnosis) of the Greater Mysteries would achieve eternal life in the hereafter. Thus, the dove or Holy Spirit perched on the Tree of Life may be a sign to the fallen Cathar Perfects of their spiritual achievement in the hereafter. Although this may be a stretch of the imagination, it seems reasonable to believe that the tarot artists were, at least in some instances, using less obvious images in their attempts to translate their messages into pictures.

The Star (Le Toule, as it is called in the Nicolas Conver deck) may also have a reference to a popular twelfth-century religious leader with a similar name, Eon de l'Etoile (d. 1150), who lived in a French town called Broceliande—a site associated with the tales of Merlin, King Arthur, and the Knights of the Round Table. De l'Etoile became an Augustinian monk and was known for his own form of magic, including being in several places at once. He was a strong critic of the wealth and worldly ways of the Roman Catholic Church. Like Robin Hood, he stole from various churches and monasteries and gave to the poor. His activities made him a popular figure among many who saw him as a messiah of sorts. In fact, it is said that the first people sent by the Church to arrest him for heresy were themselves converted by his faith.

Although comets were considered to be bad omens, de l'Etoile's name was taken from a comet that appeared in 1148. It was in that same year that Pope Eugenius III and the Council of Rheims condemned him as a heretic. Eugenius also declared that anyone aiding or abetting heretics would lose their land, and heretics who did not repent would be branded on the forehead. De l'Etoile was finally captured, tortured, and imprisoned for life. Although his followers were hunted down and burned at the stake, he remained legendary for generations to come. His legacy may have been an inspiration for many of the heretic martyrs who lived after him.

In the language of the Middle Ages, a "star" sometimes referred to the possession of an object of luck or good fortune. It was traditional in some villages, for example, to retain a lock of hair or the fingernail clippings of the dead—referred to as its "star"—in order to maintain the deceased's energy in the home.[164] In this way, we can see the association between the card and the element of good luck.

The Moon (La Lune), from the Tarot of Marseilles
by Nicolas Conver reproduced by France Cartes.

The Moon
XVIII

∽

For every one who does evil hates the light, and does
not come to the light, lest his deeds should be exposed.

—John 3:20

After The Star, we find a more ominous card where we see the moon eclipsing the sun. This image brings to mind the light of wisdom and truth (universally represented by the sun) being shadowed in darkness. In the context of our story, it reflects the difficult situation the Cathars found themselves in at the time, where secrecy and disguise became their only method of survival. It also points to the next spiritual phase in medieval cosmology.

"It is not difficult to find," writes Cirlot, "the traditional themes of the moon as the Land of the Dead or as the regenerating receptacle of souls.... Hence, for Plutarch, the souls of the just are purified in the moon, whilst their bodies return to earth and their spirit to the sun."[165] In this sense, the Moon becomes the next heavenly "pit-stop," so to speak, for the fallen Cathars after being laid to rest in The Star and before being purified in The Sun.

With card XVIII, we encounter some new and mysterious images not found in earlier tarot decks. According to Kaplan, there appears to be "no precedent in art for the Tarot of the Marseilles Moon [card]."[166] The dogs, the houses or towers, and the submerged crayfish are all novel images introduced in the Tarot of Marseilles. In an art form where everything appears to have an intended purpose, these allegorical additions to the earlier versions of the card must have a specific meaning.

The two canine-looking creatures in this card have specific references within the context of the Cathar's story. People who were unsympathetic to the Cathars were often called "dogs and wolves."[167] The Dominican friars—officers of the Inquisition— were sometimes referred to as *Domini canes*, the dogs of the Lord. Dominic's own mother was said to have seen him in a visionary dream as a dog, "barking against God's enemies."[168] When Simon de Montfort was killed, it is said that a cheer of "the wolf is dead" could be heard from the Toulousians. In addition, the heretics were often referred to as foxes "destroying the Lord's vineyards."

In The Moon, the two hound-like creatures may be the Dominicans and the Franciscans, the two monastic orders given the task of hunting down the heretics who are here depicted by the crayfish which appears to be in hiding. Cathar Perfects were known to travel at night, under the protection of darkness, in the light of the moon. As we can see, the crayfish has been drawn larger than the two canines, which may be an indication of its importance in the whole picture. However, another way to interpret these images is to see the two opposing symbols of dogs and foxes as representing the two opposing religious groups, the Cathars and the Roman Catholic Church. Upon encountering the affairs in and around Toulouse, Bernard of Clairvaux referred to the "wolves and foxes" whose words were "spreading like a canker."[169]

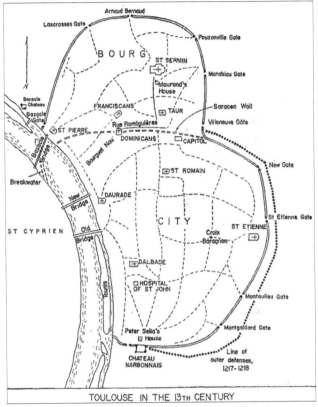

Map of Toulouse in the thirteenth century, from Walter Wakefield, Heresy, Crusade and Inquisition in Southern France, 1100-1250, University of California Press, 1974.

Another clue to The Moon might be found in examining a medieval map of Toulouse, which sits on the east bank of the Garonne River in the southwestern part of France. If we look at the town from a bird's eye view, we can see the ruins of the old Saracen wall which divided the city proper from an area called the *bourg*. These two areas were home to the two warring factions of Toulouse during the Abligensian Crusade, the White Brotherhood (established by Bishop Fulk) and the Black Brotherhood (those who opposed the Church). From a point at the river wall on the westernmost side of these Roman ruins, one could see the Dominican and Franciscan houses in the distance, located across from each other on either side of this dismantled wall. This vantage point is hauntingly similar to the perspective shown on the tarot card. Even the landscape around Toulouse is surprisingly similar to that shown on The Moon, which depicts the plains of Toulouse surrounded by the hills which border the town on both sides. These nearby mountainous regions were some of the areas where Cathars went into hiding. The man made separation of the water from the town may refer to the walls of Toulouse, which were torn down by the crusaders.

The Sun (Le Soleil), from the Tarot of Marseilles
by Nicolas Conver reproduced by France Cartes.

The Sun
XVIIII

⁓

The spiritual power was to stand related to the
temporal power as the sun to the moon.

—Pope Gregory VII, 1073

In The Sun, we have another card that has been significantly altered from its earlier versions. Instead of just a solitary image with the sun, as depicted in earlier tarot decks, we are now presented with the figures of two youths who take center stage. (In some decks, such as the Noblet Tarot, they are clearly drawn as male and female). As in the other cards of the Tarot of Marseilles, these prominent figures have a specific and intentional meaning.

Within our historical context, the two children in The Sun can very well be Jeanne, the only daughter of Count Raymond VII, and her young husband Alphonse. At the age of nine, they were promised to each other in marriage upon the signing of the Treaty of Paris of 1229. In this card, however, their union contains a positive connotation.

The peace which followed the treaty brought much needed relief to the devastated region of Toulouse. The treaty was signed on Holy Thursday, April 12—the beginning of the Easter celebration of Christ's death and resurrection. The Sun, then, is a card which marks not only the end of the house of St. Gilles (the lineage of the counts of Toulouse), but also a period of growth and renewal after twenty years of warfare. The two children are shown inside a common wall, which suggests the union of the house of St. Gilles and the French king.

The Sun is also a spiritual card, and the images of the children have important spiritual significance. For the Cathars, as for the apostles, it was essential to become childlike in order to see the world spiritually. As Jesus taught, "Unless you be converted and become as little children, you shall not enter the Kingdom of heaven" (Matthew 18:3). Of course, this was not meant to be taken literally, but rather alludes to a child's natural attributes—his innocence, vulnerability, and sense of wonder. The immediacy of a child's experience allows him to develop a faith in the world around him in contrast to the intellectual understanding of his elders. Unfettered by the restraints of his ego, the innate wisdom of the child triumphs over the knowledge of men. "The man of god, then, strives to become the Child, trusting only in god, rejecting the arrogant, falsely adult mind."[170]

If we view The Sun and The Moon through their numerology, we can catch a glimpse of their place in the tarot as dualistic principles, or opposites. The number of The Moon is 18 (1 + 8 = 9), and the number of The Sun is 19 (1 + 9 = 10, which reduces to 1—the zero being let go). Through this mathematical process, these two heavenly bodies are found at the opposite ends of the nine primary numbers. However, they appear together, one after the other, in the tarot deck. In a sense, this is the bringing together of the forces of the sun and the moon—the final resolution of opposites.

This process was known in Hermetic circles as the hieros gamos. Cirlot explains that the hieros gamos, "generally understood as the marriage of heaven and earth, may also be taken as the union of sun and moon."[171]

The hieros gamos, or marriage, of the sun and moon, from the Rosarium Philosophorum, courtesy of Deutche Fotothek. Note the vertical branch held by the dove, which creates a six-spoke wheel, representing the chi-rho, or symbol of Christ.

In medieval times, the sun symbolized spiritual matters while the moon corresponded to earthly affairs. In Catharism, the sun and the moon also represented the two major forces of the dualistic universe: lightness and darkness. As Weiss explains, "The Cathars themselves viewed their doctrine and that of the established Catholic church in just such contrasting images of light and darkness."[172] A clue to the significance of the Sun, then, may be found in this merging of dual principles (*hieros gamos*), in the "brightness" (enlightenment) which remains after false thinking is removed.

> *A book called The Everlasting Gospel, which is attributed to a mystic named Joachim, was circulated in the thirteenth century by the Spiritual Franciscans. The book was considered heretical and condemned to be burned. Nowhere did it have as much influence as it had in Languedoc. The Everlasting Gospel describes the three eras of man: the first, ruled by the Old Testament; the second, ruled by the New Testament; and the third, ruled by the Holy Spirit. Some thought that this third and final era was yet to come, while others placed its beginning in the year 1260. These three periods of time had separate corresponding heavens, each with its own unique set of images, similar to the last three astrological cards of the tarot. "The first," Lea tells us, "is like the light of the stars, the second like that of the moon, and the third like that of the sun."[173]*

In astrological terms, the two children in The Sun may represent the twins of Gemini. In medieval astrology, Gemini was symbolic of both the divine and the mortal, described as the dual principle of the "Heavenly Twin."[174] For the magician, this represents the alchemy of opposites within the self. In a spiritual sense, it is the merging of the self and the world—the transformation referred to in the section on The Magician—described by spiritualists as the point at which the ego drops away and the secrets of the world are revealed.

Occasionally, as in medieval church architecture or paintings, an artist will create clues to certain events through the use of the horoscope. If we look for astrological clues in the tarot, we might find that The Sun and The Moon are pointing to an important historical event. As Gemini is represented by the twin children on The Sun, Cancer is symbolized by the crayfish, or later the crab, on The Moon. This mystery is beyond the scope of this book, but future investigations into significant events during the sun in Gemini and the moon in Cancer may reveal significant dates in history which could add to the rich symbolism of the tarot's story. In fact, other such clues may be present in the Tarot of Marseilles, including The Star, where Venus (the woman) is found in Aquarius (the water-pourer).

Judgment (Le Jugement), from the Tarot of Marseilles
by Nicolas Conver reproduced by France Cartes.

Judgment
XX

෬

*The hour is coming in which all who are in the tombs will hear
his voice and will come out, those who have done good deeds
to the resurrection of life, but those who have done wicked deeds
to the resurrection of condemnation.*

—John 5:28

For medieval man, the Last Judgment was a real event. It
was thought to be mankind's final redemption in the Second
Coming of Christ, believed to occur in the year 1000. The Last
Judgment offered hope of salvation, and was a common theme
for preachers at the time. Until the Judgment, they taught, no
one would be allowed to enter into heaven. But when the first
millennium passed without the return of Christ, some people
began to have doubts about the plan.

One of the basic heresies of Christianity involved the
debate as to the true nature of Jesus. Was he a man, God, or a
combination of both? The Cathars believed that Christ could
not have been human, since the material body is evil. Therefore,
it follows that if Christ was not of this world, the Crucifixion
and Resurrection were also false. The Cathars believed that the
Resurrection was not to be taken literally as a specific event

in the past, but rather as an allegory of spiritual awakening in the present. In the Cathar version of the Last Judgment, the focus shifted from salvation handed down by holy proxy to one of individual responsibility. Gurevich describes this model: "Instead of a common judgment over mankind at the end of the world, a separate trial is conducted over each man."[175] This promise of personal salvation may have been one of the key factors which attracted so many to the Cathar faith. It is important to understand that the Gnostic tradition of being raised from the dead was symbolic of spiritual resurrection, and not necessarily one which supported the physical resurrection of the body after death. G.R.S. Meade explains that upon attaining a certain state of enlightenment, the Gnostic becomes "baptized" and was said to "rise from the dead."[176] At the moment of spiritual awakening, the initiate experiences his own connection to the divine. He is no longer alone and separate. He has freed himself from the Wheel of Fortune and conquered death.

The message was to receive the Holy Spirit in this life. Support for this belief can be found in early Christian writings. For example, the Gospel of Philip says, "Those who say we must die first and then rise are in error." Rather, we should "receive the resurrection whilst alive."[177] A text from one of the Nag Hammadi scrolls, the Treatise on Resurrection, states, "Why do you not examine your own self, and see that you have arisen?"[178] In the earlier Cary-Yale Tarot, the Judgment card includes a banner with the words *surgite ad judicium*, which mean "stand up" or "rise to judgment." Although this motto was omitted from later decks, the upright position of the man shown on the card suggests a message of one who has taken personal action in his spiritual rebirth. It may be useful to call on the image of The Magician here as a reference to the Hermetic version of the Judgment, in which Hermes "holds a rod in his hands, beautiful, golden, wherewith he spellbinds the eyes of men whomever he would, and wakens them again from sleep."[179]

In the Tarot of Marseilles, the middle aged man in the center of The Judgment is neither a small child, unable to understand his actions, nor an old man in fear of his death. In Toulouse, the legal age of emancipation at the time was twenty-five, when a man or woman attained a status of non-dependency. According to medieval thought, "everyone will be resurrected as a thirty year old, at the age at which Christ conquered death by rising after the crucifixion."[180] Similarly, on the tarot card, the man rises from his coffin, ready to receive the blessing of the Holy Spirit (the *consolamentum*) in the form of St. Michael, shown above in the clouds. The Cathars believed that the archangel Michael—the supreme commander in the fight against Satan—entered Mary by her right ear (as in the sound of the trumpet) and created Christ the redeemer.

The World (Le Monde), from the Tarot of Marseilles
by Nicolas Conver reproduced by France Cartes.

The World
XXI

༄

*Blessed are they which are persecuted for righteousness'
sake, for theirs is the Kingdom of Heaven.*

—Jesus, Matthew 5:10

It seems clear that The World, the last numbered card of
the major arcana, has a spiritual message to impart. In this
card we see a figure who appears to have attained spiritual
enlightenment, surrounded by the four apostles, Mark, John,
Matthew and Luke. The word "apostle" is from the Greek
apostellein, which means "to send" (as in a special message) and
from *apostolos*, "someone sent out with a message."

Like many of the other tarot cards, The World has evolved
through various changes. The shift in the imagery as it appeared
in the Tarot of Marseilles emphasizes the importance of the
gospels, represented by the four evangelists. The appearance of
the wreath may also have spiritual significance. In I Corinthians
9:24, Paul refers to working toward a Christian life as "a wreath
which will never wither." In the symbolism of the Middle Ages,
the wreath was used to denote triumph. But unlike the temporal
victory represented in The Chariot, the image here symbolizes
the final triumph of the spirit over matter.

The World, from the Visconti-Sforza tarot. Courtesy of U.S. Games Systems, Inc.

The Cathars, like the Gnostics before them, were interested in a personal truth, or *gnosis*. As was commonly done with the cardinal virtues, Truth was often depicted as a woman. We see an example of this in the revelation of Marcus, an early Christian Gnostic leader. As the story goes, Marcus envisioned a woman who revealed the truth of the universe to him.

The image of Jesus surrounded by the four apostles (associated with the "four living creatures" of the apocalypse) was common in medieval Christian art. A sculpted relief on the St. Sernin cathedral in Toulouse, for example, depicts a seated Christ in an oval wreath with the four evangelists in the corners.

The twelfth-century Chartres Cathedral has a similar relief. In fact, one would expect to see him here in his usual place "in majesty." In the Tarot of Marseilles, however, the figure of Jesus is replaced by a woman. She is holding the symbols of both man and woman (wand and conch shell), which suggests a transcendence of her sexuality. It is also possible that the figure in the center of the card is none other than the Holy Spirit, symbolized by the universal female. In a sense, this substitution of Jesus in his traditional position of majesty may suggest that the Holy Spirit was actually more significant in the minds of the creators of the Tarot of Marseilles and definitely presents a heretical twist to the traditional orthodox image.

Christ in Majesty, surrounded by the four evangelists, from the Cathedral of St. Sernin, Toulouse. Courtesy of Alison Stones.

The shift of imagery in The World from Jesus to a female figure may also suggest the importance of the Mother Goddess, who was carried over from the Gnostics. It is important to understand that there were (and still are) significant theological differences between Eastern Orthodoxy and the Church of Rome. The Eastern Orthodox Church believed that Sophia, as the divine logos, became incarnate as Jesus Christ. Sophia was the Gnostic *Anima Mundi*, the "soul of the world." Given the fact that Catharism evolved from the Eastern tradition, it follows that it may have also adopted a similar concept of the Divine Female. As Freke and Gandy explain in *The Jesus Mystery*, "Orthodox Christianity does not have a goddess. It has only God the Father, God the Son and a rather vague androgynous God the Holy Spirit. Gnostic mythology included a more natural and balanced Holy Trinity of God the Father, God the Son and the Mother Goddess, Sophia."[181] Although Sophia traditionally denotes Wisdom, Gnostic sources refer to her as a female aspect of God. She is, in effect, a lower emanation of God here on earth. In The Secret Book of John, for example, she is referred to as the "Mother" or "Mother of the Living," one of the original divine beings just below God. The text tells how Sophia created man when her offspring breathed the Spirit into him.[182]

If we look at the position of the legs of the central figure in this card, we can notice a similar crossing of one leg behind the other in The Emperor and The Hanged Man. It is possible that this was drawn this way to suggest a connection between these cards, and may refer to the traditional Christian blessing of "crossing" oneself. The connection, then, may represent a blessing of sorts from the Holy Spirit of The World to the two earlier characters in The Emperor and the Hanged Man—Count Raymond VI and his son, Raymond VII.

As we have learned from The Magician, astrology was an important science during the Middle Ages, linking man to the earth and the activities of the heavenly bodies. As the famous hermetic saying goes, "As above, so below." It should be noted that in medieval symbolism, the four evangelists are also represented by the four astrological signs of the equinox: spring (Taurus the bull); summer (Leo the lion); autumn (Scorpio, represented earlier by the eagle); and winter (Aquarius the water bearer). The four evangelists were also associated with the four elements: fire (Mark), water (John), air (Matthew), and earth (Luke).

The Fool (Le Mat), from the Tarot of Marseilles
by Nicolas Conver reproduced by France Cartes.

The Fool

0

༄

If any man among you seems to be wise, let him become
a fool that he may be wise, for the wisdom of this
world is foolishness in the eyes of God.

—Paul, 1 Corinthians 3:18-19

With this last card of the tarot—numbered 0—we have
come full circle. We have taken the journey from the trials
and tribulations of The Magician, through the events of the
Albigensian crusade and its aftermath, and now arrive at the
place of The Fool. We have also met some of the men and
women who took part in the story—the Counts of Toulouse,
Simon de Montfort, Pope Innocent III, Bishop Fulk, and the
heretic monks and Cathar Perfects. We also became familiar
with the spiritual messages of the Cathars along the way.

The Fool's number is symbolic of the circle, which represents
wholeness. As the number zero, The Fool has sometimes been
placed at the beginning of the major arcana. This might make
sense if we see him at the bottom of the social order, as he is
portrayed in other tarot decks. In the Visconti-Sforza deck, for
example, we see him as *Il Misero,* the lowly beggar. However, in
the Tarot of Marseilles, the Fool has become the Cathar Perfect

in disguise. He has reached the height of his spiritual quest and arrived at the top of the deck where he belongs. He has achieved an understanding of the spiritual messages of cards XVII through XXI—The Star, The Moon, The Sun, Judgment, and The World. He walks with his eyes uplifted to God, his clothes in tatters, unfettered by worldly possessions.

The Fool, from the Visconti-Sforza tarot. Courtesy of U.S. Games Systems, Inc.

Like most of the other cards of the major arcana, The Fool has both a spiritual and a historical message to share. Spiritually, he is the perfected Cathar, imparting his lessons of personal salvation to those willing to listen. Historically, he is the same Perfect who has found himself a fugitive from the Church, pursued by the Inquisition, in search of a new home.

In *The Cathars,* Malcolm Lambert describes the situation after the fall of Montsegur. "The Cathars would have to survive," he writes, "not by open defiance but by concealment. Rebels had to become fugitives." They became "wandering preachers, generally advocating and practicing poverty, sometimes covering considerable distances in their preaching".[183] Many of these wandering preachers were referred to as *bizoccone*, or "holy fools", like Jacopone (1236-1306) who traveled around Italy before joining the Spiritual Franciscans.[184] There was also the account of the heretic, Guilhem Raffard, who disguised himself as a beggar upon his return to Languedoc after years of exile in Italy in order to avoid detection.

The Fool may have adopted his new identity in the Tarot of Marseilles from the words of the Apostle Paul, who referred to the other apostles as "fools for Christ's sake" (1 Corinthians 4:10). The image of St. Paul's spiritual fool remained popular over the centuries. In the 1600s, the Jesuit priest, Jean-Joseph Surin, wrote, "Be a fool for God, if you want to be Holy."[185]

Because the Tarot of Marseilles is a term used to describe French tarot decks which were produced not only in Marseilles, but also in other cities like Paris and Avignon, we can expect to find variations in its style. In some decks, the name of The Fool was changed. In the Tarot of Maseilles by Conver (c. 1760), The Fool is named *le Mat*. Definitions of *mat* in the Anglo-Norman dictionary include "checkmate; beaten, [and] vanquished," all appropriate terms for the remaining Cathars after their defeat at the hands of the Church and the French crusaders.

In the older Jean Noblet deck (c. 1650), The Fool is named *Le Fou*, which is the masculine version of *Le Fol*. In the Tarot of Marseilles by Jean Dodal (c. 1701), however, The Fool is named *Le Fol*, an older version of *le folle*. *Fol* means "crazy" or "mad," but not in the sense of being insane. Rather, it has the meaning of one who may be in a fanatical state of mind, as "crazy in love." Cavendish tells us that this madness "links him not with the human but with the divine. In the ancient world," he explains, "the insane were regarded with awe because their madness showed that they were in the grip of a god or spirit. Similarly, there is an old Christian tradition of the fool as someone closer to God than other men."[186] One of the meanings given for *fol* in the Anglo-Norman dictionary is "(of religion) wicked, heretic."[187] Perhaps this was closer to the meaning of the card. Rather than disregard this variation as an error in copying or spelling, we should look at other possibilities. In the case of *Le Fol*, the suggestion might be to indicate the spiritual or even heretical connotation of The Fool. Or, since the term is in the feminine gender, it may indicate that The Fool could be a woman as well as a man. Unlike the Catholic Church, which didn't allow women in their priesthood, the Cathars had many women become prominent preachers. Although the Fool is seen wearing a beard, I think we could consider the use of the element of disguise as a factor in the appearance of this image.

Le Fol, tarot by Dodal; and Le Fou, tarot
by Noblet, photo by Jerone Charles Potts.

Another translation of the French term *le fou* is "wind-bag" or "empty bag," as in "empty-headed." It was commonly known that the Cathar Perfect carried a leather bag in which he kept his New Testament.[188] As the Fool's bag appears empty in the card, we are given a clue to his state of mind. In Cirlot's *Dictionary of Symbols*, the bag carried at the end of his staff is symbolic of his mind and its burden. Like the Buddhist monk, he has emptied himself. He is unfettered by attachments and possessions. Using Christian symbolism, we can say that he carries no cross or burden. He has learned to live outside of the drama of the Wheel of Fortune.

Buddhists and other religious groups have used the term "emptiness" to attempt to describe a type of spiritual awakening. Christian mystics have used similar terms, as when the soul becomes identical with God.[189] The image of the empty bag of The Fool may therefore refer to the Cathars' mystical experience. Unfortunately, we can not reference their actual writings on the matter to support this claim.

The position of the Fool's left arm appears odd. The bag he carries in his left hand is thrown over his right shoulder. One explanation is that in medieval art the left side is the spiritual side and the right signifies the mind. In this sense, the card may be pointing to the dominance of spirituality over the mind. Another way of looking at this is that the card may be expressing the medieval artistic tradition that the right arm "is reserved for those who suffered in the name of God."[190]

Although the Fool has attained spiritual enlightenment, he has not renounced life. His task is not done. He wanders through villages and towns in service to others, just as the apostles did—and in similar fashion to the Buddhist bodhisattva.

A similar image exists in Buddhism, as pictured in the Ten Ox-Herding Scrolls. In this series of paintings, we are shown the natural progression of spiritual attainment. It begins with a boy who finds an ox (the symbol of the mind). The next few scrolls show how the boy learns to tame the ox and live in harmony.

After attaining enlightenment, he can let go of the ox (representing the detachment of the ego) as it no longer serves a purpose. In the ninth scroll, therefore, there is nothing left but an empty circle— no ox, and no boy. However, this is not the end of the series. In the tenth and final scroll, we see the boy again, now as an older and wiser man. He has returned to normal everyday life and is pictured as a poor peasant selling his wares at the marketplace.

Image from the Ten Ox-Herding scrolls,
courtesy of the Shokoku-ji Temple.

Like the Buddhist scrolls, the tarot tells us that the spiritual enlightenment of the previous card, The World, is not the final destination. There is one more card to play. After achieving gnosis, the initiate returns to the world with a renewed sense of purpose. His task lies in the salvation of his fellow man. In the end, The Fool learns the meaning of the Buddhist saying, "Lose the Self, and gain the World."

As noted previously in The Moon, the image of the dog was often used to represent the Church. Although this image could relate to the Church in general, it could also have a specific reference. In The Fool, the image of the dog barking at the wandering Perfect may actually refer to St. Dominic, one of the major forces behind the Inquisition, who was described by his own mother as a dog "barking at heresy." A fourteenth century fresco of St. Dominic Sending Forth the Hounds of the Lord, for example, can be seen at Santa Maria Novella in Florence, Italy.

St. Dominic Sending Forth the Hounds of the Lord, with St. Peter Martyr and St. Thomas Aquinas (c. 1369) by Andrea di Bonauito, Santa Maria Novella, Florence, Italy, reproduced by permission of the Bridgeman Art Library (BAL130097).

In addition, Ladurie reminds us that in medieval times the word "dog" was commonly used as an insult.[191] In the card, we cannot help noticing the Fool's naked rear end, blatantly exposed to the dog's face. In the Jean Noblet tarot, even the

Fool's genitals are showing for all to see. Disregarding this ribald display as a random fluke would be a disservice to the artist. Instead, we should look for its meaning within the context of the reference mentioned above. This odd image can therefore be viewed as a vulgar affront by the Cathars (represented by the Fool) to the "dogs" of the Church, who they held in contempt. Just like the lampooning of a medieval political cartoon, the creators of the Tarot of Marseilles would have used this subversive image to ridicule their persecutors. In a sense, this card makes a statement of defiance: that even in the darkness of the aftermath of the Cathar repression, the Fool walks on with the knowledge that his spirit can not be conquered, but lives on in each and every one of us.

THE SPRITUAL MESSAGE:

Used as an underground textbook, the last three cards of the major arcana of the Tarot of Marseilles (Judgment, XX; The World, XXI; and The Fool, 0) might be seen as teaching the Cathar message of personal salvation. One can imagine that the early tarot storytellers—like that of the wandering preachers who went before them—might have spoken like this, as the last three cards of the major arcana were turned up:

It is possible for you to have direct knowledge of God, which is called gnosis. You do not need a priest or a church for the salvation of your soul. Simply strive to become a good person and cause no harm. You will be judged by God only, not by man. Rise up to your true nature and be filled with the Holy Spirit. It can come to you as clearly as a loud trumpet blast. Learn from the gospels, for their message is all that you need to know. Live in this world as a "fool for Christ" and follow the example of the apostles.

Denounce greed and pride and relinquish your worldly burden, including your attachment to your Self. Keep your gaze directed toward God and practice the teachings of love and compassion, even in the face of oppression. This has been passed on to you by the True Church, the Church of Love. It is the path to salvation.

Epilogue

❦

The Kingdom is inside you and outside you.... Recognize what is before your eyes, and the mysteries will be revealed to you. For there is nothing hidden that will not be revealed.... But the Kingdom of the Father is spread upon the earth and men do not see it.

—The Gospel of Thomas

The nineteenth century author, Charlotte Elizabeth, completed her book about Count Raymond of Toulouse during the last years of her life, which ended in 1846. I quote here from a section of her book in which she describes a Cathar Perfect after the Albigensian Crusade returning to what was once his homeland. Perhaps he was coming back from his years of refuge in Lombardy, where he fled from persecution. There, he would have taken asylum in the guilds of sympathizers who came to learn of the stories of the ravaging of Languedoc and the teachings of the Cathar faith. It is these stories that may have inspired some to hide the traveler's messages in the images of the tarot.

Behold that toil-worn traveler, who, in homely apparel, and with a pack of humble wares slung from his shoulders, is slowly and listlessly pursuing his way along a path once well defined and frequented, but now torn up, and well-nigh obliterated by continual alternations of the trampling march, and the utter desertion that must needs follow, where those being within reach of their grasp. He seems to know it well, and keeps so correctly within its original boundaries as to excite the attention of some few scattered laborers, who have rebuilt their ruined cots, and are tilling the deteriorated soil. These had fled to the mountain caves, or otherwise concealed themselves, while the destroying hosts swept by; and now they are again on the site of their former houses, again engaged in rural occupation, and one might hope that it is with them as in days past, when the candle of the Lord shone upon their tabernacle. The traveler is one who formerly stood conspicuous among the bold teachers of Gospel truth in that neighborhood, where pure religion was more openly countenanced, and the doctors of the faithful Church more freely encouraged than in most other places around it. He, the peddler, now bending less with age or bodily feebleness than with sorrow, had there held many a disputation with the assailants of the faith, and put to silence the subtle sophistries with which they sought to beguile the souls of his people. He had oft been the honored guest of the feudal sovereign, who ruled that province; and will was he remembered when, in his progress, but a few days since, he presented himself at the castle gate that had always been flung wide at his approach; but terror and dismay overspread the countenances of those who so readily recalled the voice and features of one concerning whom it was doubtful whether he had perished in the flames, or fallen by the sword or famine, or found a refuge in some distant clime. Word was speedily brought to the Count of the dangerous guest who stood without; and he, lately reconciled to Rome, and delivered from the ban of excommunication on a pledge of using his utmost efforts to root out every vestige of heresy wheresoever he should detect it, was for a moment in doubt whether to connive at the escape of a teacher, to whom his masters would have adjudged an abode in the deepest dungeon of the castle, with no means of prolonging life, even if that life were not publicly sacrificed to Rome. A better feeling prevailed; remembrance of the happy past, and the knowledge that the victim of persecution was a holy man, devoted to God in the Gospel of His Son, and eminently fruitful in every good word and work, restrained the unhappy noble from adding to his own sin, and to the sorrows of a helpless exile: he dispatched a knight who fully understood the matter, and participated in his feeling, to inform the wanderer that the inmates of the castle had no need of his merchandise, nor was it agreeable to their lord's will that strangers of a doubtful aspect should find admittance in these troublous times, when some evil-disposed persons were supposed to be creeping abroad, to unsettle the minds of the people, and to shake their allegiance to their sovereign lord and ruler, the vicegerent of God, the most holy and venerated pontiff.

All this was spoken, in a loud, a fierce, and a decided voice, in the hearing of those who stood near; but there was that in the old knight's eye, as, with face averted from the rest he kept it steadfastly fixed on the pastor's, which bespoke a grief and a sympathy strangely opposed both to the tenor and the tome of his speech. Touched to his inmost soul, the preacher meekly bowed submission; and with upraised eyes, silently invoking the blessing that he dared not utter aloud, he turned from the frowning battlements, to seek a lowlier shelter in the vale below.

The scattered huts among which he now passed were occupied by a race altogether unknown to him; probably adventurers from France, placed there by the wily de Montfort, to supply the lack of inhabitants where his sword had cut off every living thing. With these he sought and found a supply of his present wants; bartering the small wares of his pack for their simple fare. But ere long the scene changed, and he now finds himself among familiar faces, though intermingled with many perfectly strange. These latter were stanch and vigilant adherents to the papacy, carefully scattered about the land, to watch, and to five due notice if a symptom appeared, in public or in private, either of the retention or revival of heresy in any form whatever.

With an overflowing heart does that beloved teacher approach the objects of his former care; and quickly is he recognized, as the deep pantings of many a bosom declared, while the brow perchance is knitted, to discourage, and the head bent or the eye averted, to shun him. There is no sign of welcome, no whispering salutation of peace: nothing but an evident dread, lest his presence should lead to their destruction. By some, the crucifix is hastily displayed, as a token that, before man at least, they know no better hope than such lying vanities can impart; and others, by a loud remark to a neighboring assistant, convey the intimation that their creed is that which of old they abjured.

Meanwhile, a group of children, and very young persons, gather around the traveler, demanding to see the contents of his pack, which he readily spreads before them; gazing with wistful curiosity in their blooming faces, touched as some among them were with traces of early suffering, and more than one or two exhibiting scars from the cuts of a merciless sabre. Among those who bent over the scattered treasures, he is struck by the countenances of two lovely girls, twins, whose close resemblance to each other is scarcely greater than what both bear to a peasant who was once the very flower of his flock in that district; and well he remembers baptizing twin girls of hers some ten years previously, and sweet is the recollection of the season of prayer and praise that marked the event. A longing desire to hear of her, half subdued by fear lest the tale of apostasy should blight his once confident hope in the firm faith of that devoted woman, leads him to watch every movement of the lively twins, until at length one of them, selecting an article, holds it up, demanding its price. As she shakes back the wild ringlet from her brow, the resemblance becomes more striking; and he answers her inquiry, adding, 'If your mother, young maiden, approves the purchase, we shall not dispute about the price.' 'What know you of her mother?' asked a sinister-looking young man who stood by: and the teacher, fearing for these lambs of a broken fold, replies, 'I know not even their names, or yours, or any around me: but the young should seek to be guided by parental wisdom, even in trifling things.' 'She has no mother, happily for her!' was the remark of several of the bystanders: and the girl herself hastily added, 'My mother was burnt with fifteen other heretics, by the holy pilgrims, four ears ago.' 'And we are good Catholics, and hate all heresy,' said the other twin.

This little incident told a tale more comprehensive, more heart-rendering, than many a day's investigation might have done. The children spoke, evidently in some terror: and the very tome in which their remarks were made proved them to have been learned by rote.

The peddler gathered his wares up, after disposing of a few, and crossing in heavy silence the vineyard, he perceived the father of the twins engaged at his work. Resolved to discover some ground of consolation here, he neither approached him nor attracted his attention: but seeking present rest in a secluded corner, awaited the close of day; then to seek the humble dwelling where his heart told him he should find the wonted welcome.

He went: the father was seated in his hut, and around him the few children left of a large family, one of whom was crippled and helpless from the effects of savage cruelty. The teacher entered, and threw off his slouching cap, and stood fully revealed, prepared to fold in a paternal embrace these objects of his solicitous care. The father sprang form his seat, and with frantic gesture, in tones of wild, but smothered passion, exclaimed, 'Begone! Begone! Is it not yet enough? Has not the flame been fed? Has not the sword been glutted? Has not the rack enjoyed its prey? Come you here to mark out the victims anew, to let loose the blood-hounds - the holy pilgrims - the crusaders - on a ravaged district? Begone to your concealment, be it where it may; and God help you safe back to it! But leave us, leave the place, we are changed now: we are loyal to - begone!'

It was enough: the pastor's cup of sorrow was full. Farther search he deemed fruitless for any good effect, and pregnant with peril to his lost flock. He turned, prepared to retrace his steps to the place of his distant refuge, where, in rocks and caves, were hidden a smaller band of fugitives to whose persevering entreaties, and almost violence, he owed his own safety. Sad were the tidings he must bear to them, of many whom he had seen under circumstances that scarcely allowed a hope to linger in his breast, as to their fidelity to the faith; but he cast himself on the firm rock of Christ's word, in reference to such as were truly his sheep – I give unto them eternal life, and none is able to pluck them out of my hand;' and thus, sorrowful, yet always rejoicing, he pursued the pathway home.[192]

Bibliography

❧

Adams, Henry. *Mont-Saint-Michel and Chartres*. New York: The Heritage Press, 1957.

Allshorn, Lionel. *Stupor Mundi, The Life and Times of Frederick II Emperor of the Romans King of Sicily and Jerusalem 1194-1250*. London: Martim Secker, 1912.

Barber, Malcolm. *The Two Cities: Medieval Europe 1050–1320*. London: Routledge, 1992.

Barnstone, Willis (editor). *The Other Bible*. San Francisco: Harper and Row, 1984.

Biller, Peter and Hudson, Anne (editors). *Heresy and Literacy, 1000-1530*. New York: Cambridge University Press, 1994.

Bishop, Morris. *The Middle Ages*. New York: American Heritage, 1968.

Blakeley, John. *The Mystical Tower of the Tarot*. London: Robinson and Watkins, 1974.

Boethius, *Consolation of Philosophy*, Victor Watts (translator). London: Penguin Books, 1969.

Cahill, Thomas. *Mysteries of the Middle Ages, the Rise of Feminism, Science and Art from the Cults of Catholic Europe*. New York: Doubleday, 2006.

Campbell, Joseph and Richard Roberts. *Tarot Revelations*. San Anselmo, CA: Vernal Equinox Press, 1979.

Case, Paul Foster. *The Tarot: A Key to the Wisdom of the Ages.* New York: Macoy Publishing Co., 1947.

Cavendish, Richard. *The Tarot.* London: Chancellor Press, 1986.

Cheyette, Fredric. *Ermengard of Narbonne and the World of the Troubadours.* Ithica, New York: Cornell University Press, 2001.

Cirlot, J. E. *A Dictionary of Symbols.* New York: Philosophical Library, 1962.

Crowley, Aleister. *The Book of Thoth.* York Beach, ME: Samuel Weiser, Inc., 1969.

Douglas, Alfred. *The Tarot: The Origins, Meaning and Uses of the Cards.* New York: Penguin Books, 1972.

Dummett, Michael. *The Visconti-Sforza Tarot Cards.* New York: George Braziller, 1986.

Elizabeth, Charlotte. *Count Raymond of Toulouse and the Crusade Against the Albigensians under Pope Innocent III.* New York: M.W. Dodd, 1851.

Erickson, Carolly. *The Medieval Vision: Essays in History and Perception.* London: Oxford University Press, 1976.

Ferguson, George. *Signs and Symbols in Christian Art.* New York: Oxford University Press, 1954.

Freeman, Charles. *The Closing of the Western Mind.* New York: Vintage Books, 2005.

Freke, Timothy and Paul Gandy. *The Jesus Mysteries.* New York: Three Rivers Press, 1999.

Garin, Eugenio. *Astrology in the Renaissance: The Zodiac of Life.* London: Routledge and Kegan Paul, 1983.

Gettings, Fred. The Secret Zodiac, The Hidden Art in Medieval Society. London: Routledge & Kegan Paul, 1987.

Giles, Cynthia. *The Tarot: History, Mystery and Lore.* New York: Paragon House, 1992.

Gregory, Stewart, William Rothwell and David Trotter (editors). *Anglo-Norman Dictionary, 2nd ed.* London: Maney Publishing, 2005.

Gurevich, Aron. *Medieval Popular Culture: Problems of Belief and Perception*, translated by Janos Bak and Paul Hollingsworth. Cambridge: Cambridge University Press, 1990.

Haskins, Charles. *The Renaissance of the 12th Century.* Cleveland: Meridian Books, 1957.

Heath, Sidney. *The Romance of Symbolism and its Relation to Church Ornament and Architecture.* London: Francis Griffiths, 1909.

Hopkins, Marilyn. *The Enigma of the Knights Templar, Their History and Mystical Connections.* New York: The Disinformation Company, 2007.

Huson, Paul. *The Devil's Picture Book.* New York: Berkeley Publishing Co., 1970.

———. *Mystical Origins of the Tarot.* Vermont: Destiny Books, 2004.

Kaplan, Stuart. *The Encyclopedia of Tarot.* New York: U.S. Games Systems, 1978.

———. *The Encyclopedia of Tarot, Vol. II.* Stamford, CT: U.S. Games, 1986.

Katzenellenbogen, Adolf. *Allegories of the Virtues and Vices in Medieval Art.* New York: W.W. Norton & Co, 1964.

Krey, A. C. *The First Crusade: Accounts of Eye-Witnesses and Participants*. Princeton: Princeton University Press, 1921.

Ladurie, Emmanuel LeRoy. *Montaillou, The Promised Land of Error*. New York: Vintage Books, 1979.

Lambert, Malcolm. *The Cathars*. Malden, MA: Blackwell Publishing, 1998.

Lea, Henry, *The History of the Inquisition of the Middle Ages*. New York: Harbor Press, 1955.

Lewis, C. S. *The Discarded Image: An Introduction to Medieval and Renaissance Literature*. Cambridge: Cambridge University Press, 1964.

Logan, F. Donald. *The History of the Church in the Middle Ages*. New York: Routledge, 2002.

Mâle, Emile. *The Gothic Image: Religious Art in France of the Thirteenth Century*. New York: Harper Brothers, 1958.

Manchester, William. *A World Lit Only by Fire: The Medieval Mind and the Renaissance, Portrait of an Age*. Boston: Little, Brown & Co., 1992.

Madaule, Jacques. *The Albigensian Crusade*. London: Burns and Oats, 1967.

May, Rollo. *Symbolism in Religion and Literature*. New York: George Braziller, 1960.

McGinn, Bernard. *The Flowering of Mysticism, Men and Women in the New Mysticism—1200-1350*. New York: The Crossroad Publishing Co., 1998.

Meade, G.R.S. *Fragments of a Faith Forgotten: The Gnostics: A Contribution to the Study of the Origins of Christianity*. New York: University Books, Inc., 1960.

Meyer, Marvin, translator. *The Secret Teachings of Jesus: Four Gnostic Gospels*. New York: Vintage Books, 1986.

Mundy, J.H. *Society and Government at Toulouse in the Age of the Cathars*. Toronto: Pontifical Institute of Medieval Studies, 1997.

———. *The Repression of Catharism at Toulouse: The Royal Diploma of 1279*. Toronto: Pontifical Institute of Medieval Studies, 1985.

Murray, Peter and Linda. *Oxford Dictionary of Christian Art*. New York: Oxford University Press, 1996.

Nichols, Sallie. *Jung and the Tarot: An Archetypal Journey*. York Beach, ME: Samuel Weiser, 1980.

Oldenbourgh, Zoe. *Massacre at Montsegur: A History of the Albigensian Crusade*. New York: Dorsett Press, 1990.

O'Neill, Robert. *Tarot Symbolism*. Lima, OH: Fairway Press, 1986.

O'Reilly, Elizabeth Boyle. *How France Built Her Cathedrals*. New York: Harper and Brothers, 1921.

O'Shea, Stephen. *The Perfect Heresy: The Revolutionary Life and Death of the Medieval Cathars*. New York: Walker and Company, 2000.

Pagels, Elaine. *The Gnostic Gospels*. New York: Vintage Books, 1989.

———. Beyond Belief, *The Secret Gospel of Thomas*. New York: Vintage Books, 2003.

Papus, *The Tarot of the Bohemians: The Absolute Key to Occult Science*. Translated by A. P. Morton. No. Hollywood, CA: Wilshire Book Co., 1978.

Payne-Towler, Christine. *The Underground Stream: Esoteric Tarot Revealed*. Oregon: Noreah Press, 1999.

Phillips, Jonathan. *Holy Warriors: A Modern History of the Crusades*. New York: Random House, 2009.

Pollack, Rachel. *Seventy-Eight Degrees of Wisdom: A Book of Tarot*. London: Harper Collins, 1980.

Roach, Andrew. *The Devil's World: Heresy and Society 1100-1300*. United Kingdom: Pearson Education, 2005.

Runciman, Steven. *The Medieval Manichee, A Study of the Christian Dualist Heresy*. London: Cambridge University Press, 1960.

Sadhu, Mouni. *The Tarot*. No. Hollywood, CA: Wilshire Book Co., 1971.

Saward, John. *Perfect Fools*. London: Oxford University Press, 1980.

Sekules, Veronica. *Medieval Art*. New York: Oxford University Press, 2001.

Seznec, Jean. *The Survival of the Pagan Gods, The Mythological Tradition and its Place in Renaissance Humanism and Art*. New Jersey: Princeton University Press, 1981.

Shinners, John (ed.). *Medieval Popular Religion 1000-1500: A Reader*. New York: Broadview Press, 1997.

Shirley, Janet (translator). *The Song of the Cathar Wars, A History of the Albigensian Crusade*. Burlington, VT: Ashgate Publishing, 1996.

Sibly, W. A. and M. D, Sibly, translators. *The History of the Albigensian Crusade, Peter of les Vaux-de-Cernay*. Woodbridge, U.K.: Boydell Press, 1998.

_____. *The Chronicle of William of Puylaurens*. Woodbridge, U.K.: Boydell Press, 2003.

Starbird, Margaret. *The Tarot Trumps and the Holy Grail, Great Secrets of the Middle Ages*. Boulder, CO: Woven Word Press, 2000.

Sumption, Jonathan. *The Albigensian Crusade*. London: Faber and Faber, 1978.

Tuchman, Barbara. *A Distant Mirror*. New York: Ballantine Books, 1978.

Versluis, Arthur. *The Philosophy of Magic*. Boston: Routledge & Kegan Paul, 1986.

Waite, A. E. *The Pictorial Key to the Tarot*. New York: Dover Publications, Inc., 2005.

Wakefield, Walter. *Heresy, Crusade and Inquisition in Southern France, 1100-1250*. Berkeley: University of California Press, 1974.

Wakefield, Walter L. and Evans, Austin P., *Heresies of the High Middle Ages*, New York: Columbia University Press, 1969.

Walker, D. P. *Spiritual and Demonic Magic: From Ficino to Campanella*. University Park, PA: Pennsylvania State University Press, 2000.

Warner, H. J. *The Albigensian Heresy (Vols. I & II)*. New York: Russell & Rusell, 1967.

Weis, Rene. *The Yellow Cross: The Story of the Last Cathars, 1290-1329*. New York: Alfred A. Knopf, 2001.

Wirth, Oswald. *The Tarot of the Magicians*. York Beach, ME: Samuel Weiser, Inc., 1985.

Yates, Frances. *Giordano Bruno and the Hermetic Tradition*. Chicago: University of Chicago Press, 1964.

Notes

ᗣ

1   Alfred Douglas, *The Tarot*, p. 27.

2   Camoin.com

3   Emile Mâle, *The Gothic Image*, p.22.

4   Donald Logan, *History of the Church in the Middle Ages*, p.136.

5   Bernard McGinn, *The Flowering of Mysticism*, p.4.

6   Jonathan Phillips, *Holy Warriors*, p.199.

7   Walter Wakefield, *Heresies of the High Middle Ages*, p. 40.

8   Paul Huson, *The Devil's Picture Book*, pp. 67-68.

9   Cynthia Giles, *The Tarot, History, Mystery and Lore*, p. 65.

10 Jonathan Sumption, *The Albigensian Crusade*, p. 47.

11 Charles Haskins, *The Renaissance of the 12ᵗʰ Century*, p. 349.

12 Malcolm Barber, *The Two Cities, Medieval Europe 1050-1320*, p. 440.

13 Morris Bishop, *The Middle Ages,* p. 276.

14 Stuart Kaplan, *The Encyclopedia of Tarot,* vol. I, p. 35.

15 Richard Cavendish, *The Tarot,* p. 18.

16 *Ibid.* p. 16.

17 A.E. Waite, *The Pictorial Key to the Tarot*, p. 3.

18 Kaplan, *The Encyclopedia of Tarot,* vol. II, p. 270.

19 Robert O'Neill, *Tarot Symbolism*, p. 201.

20 Andrew Roach, *The Devil's World*, p. 210.

21 Emanuel Ladurie, *Montaillou*, p. 26.

22 Huson, *Mystical Origins of the Tarot*, p.33.

23 O'Neill, p. 210.

24 Aron Gurevich, *Medieval Popular Culture*, p. 123.

25   Giles, p. 25.

26   Logan, p. 235.

27   *Ibid*. p.299.

28   Henry Lea. *The History of the Inquisition of the Middle Ages*, vol. I, p. 47.

29   Barbara Tuchman, *A Distant Mirror,* p. 34.

30   Carolly Erickson, *The Medieval Vision,* p. 97.

31   Elizabeth O'Reilly, *How France Built Her Cathedrals*, p.64.

32   Lea, vol. I, p. 6.

33   *Ibid*. p. 35.

34   *Ibid*. p. 67.

35   H. J. Warner, *The Albigensian Heresy*, vol. II, p. 106.

36   Sumption, p. 18.

37   W. A. Sibly, and M. D. Sibly (translators), *The History of the Albigensian Crusade,* p. 22.

38   Zoe Oldenbourgh, *Massacre at Montsegur,* p. 50.

39   H.J. Warner, *The Albigensian Heresy*, vol. II, p. 62.

40   Mark Gregory Pegg, *A Most Holy War*, p. 40.

41   Fredric Cheyette, *Ermengard*, p. 286.

42   Rene Weis, *The Yellow Cross,* p. xxvi.

43   J. H. Mundy, *The Repression of Catharism at Toulouse*, p. 14.

44   Jaques Madaule, *The Albigensian Crusade*, pp. 52-53.

45   Sibly and Sibly, *The Chronicle of William Puylaurens*, p. 25.

46   Lea, vol. I, p. 107.

47   Cheyette, p. 298.

48   Peter Biller, *Heresy and Literacy* p.52.

49   McGinn, vol. I, p. 79.

50   Warner, p. 71.

51   Steven Runciman, *The Medieval Manichee*, p. 154.

52   *Ibid*. p. 154.

53 Wakefield, *Heresies of the High Middle Ages*, p.21.

54 *Ibid*. p. 5.

55 Erickson, p. 95.

56 Ladurie, p. 81.

57 Wakefield, p.28.

58 Phillips, p.203.

59 Sibly and Sibly, *The Chronicle of William of Puylaurens*, p. 128.

60 Madaule, pp. 72-73.

61 Lea, vol. II, p. 43.

62 Emmanuel Ladurie, *Montaillou*, p. xi.

63 Lea, vol. I, p. 395.

64 Malcolm Lambert, *The Cathars*, p. 283.

65 *Ibid*. p. 83.

66 Roach, p.122.

67 Biller, p.57.

68 Wakefield, *Heresies of the High Middle Ages*, p. 41.

69 *Ibid*. p. 393.

70 *Ibid*. p. 313.

71 Ibid. p. 330.

72 Roach, p. 155.

73 Warner, vol. II, p. 209.

74 Lambert, p. 289.

75 Thomas Cahill, *Mystery of the Middle Ages* p.231.

76 Lea, vol. II, p. 56.

77 Wakefield, *Heresy, Crusade and Inquisition*, p. 224.

78 Charlotte Elizabeth, *Count Raymond*, p. 290.

79 Lea, vol. I, p. 321.

80 Stephen O'Shea, *The Perfect Heresy*, p. 223.

81 Kaplan, vol. II, p.53.

[82] O'Neill, *Catharism and the Tarot, Tarot.com/about-tarot/library.boneill/*

[83] Veronica Sekules, *Medieval Art*, p. 56.

[84] Kaplan, vol. I, p. 345.

[85] Giles, p. 44.

[86] Sidney Heath, *The Romance of Symbolism*, p.10.

[87] Mâle, p.1.

[88] *Ibid.* p.10.

[89] Giles, p. 7.

[90] Biller, p. 62.

[91] O'Neill, *Catharism and the Tarot Part III, Tarot.com.*

[92] Lea, vol. III, p. 624.

[93] Arthur Versluis, *The Philosophy of Magic*, p. 18.

[94] Frances Yates, *Giordano Bruno and the Hermetic Tradition*, p. 111.

[95] Ladurie, p. 296.

[96] Huson, *The Devil's Picture Book*, p. 87.

[97] Wakefield, *Heresy, Crusade and Inquisition*, p. 66.

[98] Mundy, *The Repression of Catharism at Toulouse*, p. 25.

[99] Warner, p. 86.

[100] Mâle, p.32.

[101] Pagels, *The Gnostic Gospels*, p. 65.

[102] John Shinners, *Medieval Popular Religion,* p.26.

[103] McGinn, p. 15.

[104] Runciman, p. 132.

[105] O'Shea, p. x.

[106] Sumption, p. 56.

[107] Shinners, pp. 113-115.

[108] Janet Shirley, *The Song of the Cathar Wars*, p. 179.

[109] Henry Adams, *Mont-Saint-Michel and Chartres*, p. 87.

[110] Shinners, p.116.

111 Warner, vol. I, p. 32.

112 Ladurie, p. 63.

113 Cavendish, p. 76.

114 Sekules, p. 13.

115 Lionel Allshorn, *Stupor Mundi*, p. 234.

116 Cahill, p. 278.

117 *Ibid.* p. 278.

118 Logan, p. 185.

119 Allshorn, p. 32.

120 *Ibid.* p. 84.

121 J. E. Cirlot, *A Dictionary of Symbols*, p. 88.

122 Bishop, p. 271.

123 O'Neill, p. 205.

124 Cirlot, p. 258.

125 Runciman, p. 162.

126 Cahill, p. 311.

127 Christine Payne-Towler, *The Underground Stream*, p.27.

128 Mâle, p.11.

129 Wakefield, *Heresies of the High Middle Ages*, p.396.

130 Sekules, p. 133.

131 Tuchman, p. 16.

132 Roach, p. 80.

133 Wakefield, *Heresy, Crusade and Inquisition*, p. 24.

134 Cheyette, p. 288.

135 Boethius, *Consolation of Philosophy*, Watts (trans.), Book VI, ch. 3.

136 Warner, vol. II, p. 119.

137 Sibly and Sibly, *The Chronicle of William of Puylaurens*, p. 42.

138 Tuchman, p. 11.

139 Lea, vol. II, p. 22.

140 Lea, vol I, p. 208.

141 *Ibid.* vol. I, p. 203.

142 *Ibid.* p. 206.

143 Mâle, p.11.

144 Shirley, p. 180.

145 A. C. Krey, *The First Crusade*, p. 262.

146 Sibly and Sibly, *Peter of Les Vaux-de-Cernay*, p. 117.

147 *Ibid.* p. 70.

148 Charlotte Elizabeth, *Count Raymond*, p. 102.

149 George Ferguson, *Signs and Symbols in Christian Art*, p. 183.

150 Ladurie, p. 288.

151 *Ibid.* p. 32.

152 *Ibid.* p. xiii.

153 *Ibid.* p. 13.

154 *Ibid.* p. 13.

155 Oldenbourg, p. 95.

156 Pegg, p. 15

157 Wakefield, *Heresy, Crusade and Inquisition*, p. 60.

158 Kaplan, vol. II, p. 11.

159 J. H. Mundy, *Society and Government in Toulouse in the Age of the Cathars*, p. 121.

160 Cavendish, p. 21.

161 Bishop, pp. 160-161.

162 Shirley, p.123.

163 Cirlot, p. 81.

164 Ladurie, p. 31.

165 Cirlot, p. 205.

166 Kaplan, vol. II, p. 176.

167 Lambert, p. 265.

168 Oldenbourg, p. 237.

169 Roach, p.69.

170 John Saward, *Perfect Fools*, p. 64.

171 Cirlot, p. 204.

172 Weiss, p. xxiii.

173 Lea, vol. III, p. 21.

174 Cirlot, p. 111.

175 Aron Gurevich, *Medieval Popular Culture*, p. 120.

176 G. R. S. Meade, *Fragments of a Faith Forgotten: the Gnostics*, p. 176.

177 Pagels, *The Gnostic Gospels*. p. 12.

178 *Ibid*. p. 12.

179 Meade, p. 201.

180 Gurevich, p. 105

181 Timothy Freke and Paul Gandy, *The Jesus Mysteries*, p. 98.

182 Marvin Meyer., *Secret Teachings of Jesus*, p. 79.

183 Lambert, p. 169.

184 McGinn, p. 125.

185 Saward, p. 137.

186 Cavendish, p. 59.

187 Gregory, Rothwell and Trotter, *Anglo-Norman Dictionary*, 2nd ed.

188 Runciman, p. 160.

189 McGinn, p. 129.

190 Mâle, p.6.

191 Ladurie, p. 290.

192 Elizabeth, pp. 223-229.

Index

❧

251

Made in the USA
Lexington, KY
01 May 2012